20TH CENTURY ROCK AND ROLL
WOMEN IN ROCK

Dale Sherman

Edit and additional research by Steve Whitfield

Table Of Contents

20TH CENTURY ROCK AND ROLL

WOMEN IN ROCK

Dale Sherman

WATCH FOR THE REST OF THE SERIES

A GUIDE TO THE ARTISTS WHO MADE THE CENTURY'S GREATEST ROCK MUSIC

20th CENTURY ROCK AND ROLL

A COLLECTOR'S GUIDE PUBLISHING SERIES

Psychedelia	ISBN 1-896522-40-8
Alternative Music	ISBN 1-896522-19-X
Progressive Rock	ISBN 1-896522-20-3
Heavy Metal	ISBN 1-896522-47-5
Pop Music	ISBN 1-896522-25-4
Punk Rock	ISBN 1-896522-27-0
Glam Rock	ISBN 1-896522-26-2
Women In Rock	ISBN 1-896522-29-7

For ordering information see our web site at
www.cgpublishing.com

We acknowledge the financial support of the Government of Canada through
the Book Publishing Industry Development Program for our publishing activities.
Published by Collector's Guide Publishing Inc., Box 62034, Burlington, Ontario, Canada, L7R 4K2
Printed and bound in Canada
20th Century Rock and Roll - Women In Rock
by Dale Sherman
ISBN 1-896522-29-7

Table Of Contents

Acknowledgments

Just brief tips of the hat to the many people who helped (or wanted to help) with the creation of this book. Once people found out that I was writing a book about women in rock music, everyone seemed to have immediate suggestions as to who should be covered and why. In some cases I was convinced to include women that I otherwise would not have thought of. In other cases I found that I had to forego selecting some for reasons given to me. Either way, having only so much room will no doubt leave some friends and corespondents frustrated by not seeing their favorites here. Please accept my apologies. Then again, maybe that'll be a good reason for a second volume someday.

Special thanks must go to those who helped out with material that I didn't have readily available to me, including Carlyn Nugent, Becca Stocker, Steve LaDuke and David Miller. I must also extend additional thanks to David Miller for his work on the Judy Tudzke article in the book. David had to convince me to include Judy, and did so with an argument so well written that he agreed to my just restructuring his argument a bit and using it as the essay on Judy that appears herein. While I wrote all of the other essays, I can't complete the book without mentioning David's involvement and my gratitude for his assistance.

I also must thank my wife, Jill, for her dedication to the project. Jill worked hard on tracking down books, articles and web site information about the artists — sometimes to the point of having enough research material to write individual books on each artist instead of just short essays. It would have been twice as hard to complete the book without her.

Thanks to the people at CGP for allowing me a chance to write outside of the box. Much appreciated. Finally, thanks to all the women in music — for their talent, their creativity and their ability to make me a fan — then, now and yet to come.

Picture Credits

courtesy Hot Wacks
"The Bootleg Expert"
The Hot Wacks Press
P.O. Box 544, Owen Sound,
Ontario, Canada N4K 6J9

courtesy Rock Classics
© Rock Classics

courtesy KAOS2000
© Phil Anderson /
KAOS2000 Magazine
www.kaos2000.net

Front cover pictures © Phil Anderson

~ Introduction ~

"Girls can't play Rock and Roll!"

I can't tell you how many times I've heard that comment over the years — normally from guys who've never played a musical instrument in their lives. Then again, women say it as well, and most of them saying it haven't picked up a musical instrument either, so it's not just the guys that are wrong.

Of course, it's easy to just look at the statement and think, "what an ignorant thing to say." One could also say it's sexist, but "ignorance" covers the ground nicely — they simply don't know what they're talking about. What I think it really demonstrates about the man who says it is that they have no notion, not even a clue, as to what REAL Rock and Roll is about.

Sure, there are those who'll tell you that sex is the metaphor of rock music. Which is understandable, as some of the most popular songs from the past fifty years have involved sex in one fashion or another. Most probably, that's why these guys get so uptight about seeing a woman (or women) up on stage — they feel it's no place for a woman unless she's a stripper.

Yet, sex is just one topic in rock music. It's not the focus. The true roots of Rock and Roll are in rebellion. It's in the ability to set one's thoughts down in a fashion that makes you want to stand up, scream out, raise a fist in the air and dance. It's supposed to be unsettling; Make you move; Make you react; Make you sweat; Make you THINK? Hmmm . . . maybe, but let's not take the fun out of this.

Southern rock; punk rock; hard rock; alternative rock; new wave rock — the key word here is Rock. And no matter how it's been affected by the turn of the generations, it's still a form of rebellion that you can dance to (be it the Twist or diving in the mosh-pit). It's supposed to scare parents and worry the preacher. It makes kids feel good.

So when a woman picks up that guitar, or plays the drums, or just belts out a song, it's not just to impress the guys. Who cares about the guys? Most of them are not up there to impress the guys (unlike the guys who are there mainly to impress the girls). The women are playing because they want to play. They want to rebel against the norm of what's expected of them (be it from Mom and Dad or the boy next door). They just want to rock.

They will and they have.

Looking back at the past few decades, many rock fans will instantly remember some of the male bands or performers that they've listened to who. But no one, not even the most chauvinistic of the bunch, will deny that there's at least one woman artist about which they found themselves thinking, "yeah, she was cool." This book is about these women: the ones who helped create rock music over the past fifty years; the ones without whom rock music wouldn't be what it is today.

It's not just a failure of the fans, but of the critics as well. How many books are out there about women in music? Several, although you may have to search for them. Fine and good. It's a topic that deserves as many books as possible. But how often have the books been solely about women in rock music? Pretty rare, actually. Oh sure, most of the books cover some of the more popular artists, but for every book that covers Patti Smith or Janis Joplin, Dolly Parton or Olivia Newton-John appear as well. Rockers? Sure, they could rock out when they wanted to, but, c'mon, rockers?

Why has this been the case? It's simple — authors of books about music and musicians tend to look at women in music as a separate genre unto itself. By doing so, they segregate the women into a field all their own where you have Dolly Parton competing against Wendy O. Williams, or Celine Dion against Joan Jett. In wanting to praise the accomplishments of these artists, the writers end up stereotyping the whole lot as a single group — shaped to form a collective ideal or thought instead of being individuals expressing their own ideas. But these women can be as independent, and as different from each other as from any male performer. By trying to shine a spotlight on these talents, the writers end up only showcasing their own understanding (or lack of) when it comes to women in rock music.

So that's why this book is not an all encompassing volume of women in music. It's not even a look at all of the women in rock music. Instead, it's a look at 50 women rockers who have helped to shape, in one form or another, the entire world of rock music, and not just the little corner normally relegated to women in rock. Some of those listed here could be argued as being on the edge of the rock genre, but all contributed something to rock music styles.

And it's not just the women solo artists we'll look at — there's the girl groups, the all female bands (that've had hit after hit), and the bands that aren't complete without that one particular woman as the "front man." They're here as well. And after you've read this entire book, we'll still be a long way from having looked at all of the women rock performers out there.

So the next time you hear some guy bellowing about how women can't rock, just think about the women in this book, and know that our loud-mouthed expostulater must be a failure in the Rock and Roll world.

Better yet, just take a copy of this book and glue it to his forehead. It'll give him something to read while he's trying to figure out why nobody likes him.

~ 1 ~
Tori Amos

As the 1990's began, the alternative rock movement was in full force, thanks to the investments made by college and alternative rock radio stations into the grunge genre, and the general need of teenagers for a musical style that separated them from the masses. With the mid- to late-1980's following a line of more and more progressive orchestrations in music (which was probably the death blow to the heavy metal movement), the alternative genre expressed a more basic, stripped down sound and an emphasis on lyrics over orchestrations.

For the most part, this lead to a cross-pollination of metal and punk, but in some cases it lead to a more mellow type of music in the 90's than what had been appearing in the 80's. These circumstances helped performers who were devoted to playing their own music, and were also trying to say something in their lyrics beyond the obvious. For Tori Amos, it was the perfect time to pick up the pieces of an earlier attempt in metal and try to go in her own direction.

courtesy Rock Classics

Born Myra Ellen Amos in Newton, North Carolina on August 22, 1963, Tori had was learning the piano at the age of two. Because of her abilities, her parents had the foresight to enroll her into the Peabody Conservatory in Baltimore, Maryland at the age of five. All was fine and good there until the age of eleven when it was discovered that she was playing by ear instead of reading the music and she was dropped from the Conservatory.

This public setback, however, didn't stop Tori Amos from continuing to make music and she released her first single (*Baltimore*) in 1980 on her own label. After sending out demo tapes to a variety of people in the industry, Amos finally moved to Los Angeles in 1985 to get closer to the music business. It was there that Amos took the name Tori and in 1987 she finally landed a contract with the Atlantic Records label. This lead to her first album — which, unfortunately, was a disappointment, both artistically and financially.

Y KANT TORI READ, a pseudo-metal rock group, with Tori as the scantily clad front singer, went nowhere quickly and faded from view even faster. Although it's considered a collector's item for Tori Amos fans, the only positive thing that came out of the recordings for the album was that Tori realized she needed a change in approach if she was going to make it on her own. Working as a backup singer on a variety of projects, Tori moved to London, England in 1991 and began investigating other musical directions.

courtesy Rock Classics

In London that she discovered that her first love, the piano, was the best new element that she could bring to her music and began etching out a new career using the piano as the main orchestration in her music. Combined with the abstract, poetic quality of her lyrics, her music began being compared to that of artists like Joni Mitchell and Kate Bush. With a set of songs already in place, Atlantic obliged with the recording of another album in Tori's contract and late 1991 saw the release of LITTLE EARTHQUAKES.

The album did well on both sides of the Atlantic (no pun intended), and Tori began touring in support of the album. By the end of 1992 she was voted "Best New Female Artist" by the readers of Rolling Stone magazine and she was ready to begin work on a follow-up album, which took most of 1993 to write and record. This album, UNDER THE PINK, went straight to No. 1 in the UK and reach No. 12 in the US, a surprising leap from just five years before when Y KANT TORI READ didn't even make a dent in the charts.

Her lyrics and melodies continued win over listeners to her music, especially in the way her poetry wove stories through the music. This was the style that she followed (and progressed with) right through the three successful albums that she's released since that time.

And in doing so, Tori Amos became one of the first artists of the new rock movement of the 1990's, and her musical styles were picked up by other artists — male and female alike — during the 1990's. As for Tori's brief journey into metal, it's a prime example of how a record company can invest in a wrong persona for a performer, and how it was up to the artist herself to find another direction to success in the long run. As will be seen, this was just one case of many.

Selected Studio Albums:
  ◦ Y CANT TORI READ (Atlantic, 1987)
  ◦ LITTLE EARTHQUAKES (Atlantic, 1991)
  ◦ UNDER THE PINK (Atlantic, 1994)
  ◦ BOYS FOR PELE (Atlantic, 1996)
  ◦ FROM THE CHOIRGIRL HOTEL (Atlantic, 1998)
  ◦ TO VENUS AND BACK (Atlantic, 1999)

Best of the "Best Of" Albums:
  ◦ MAXIMUM TORI (2000)

~ 2 ~
Laurie Anderson

Born June 5, 1947 in Chicago, Illinois, Laura Anderson began playing the violin as a child and eventually joined the Chicago Youth Symphony before moving to New York to study art history at Barnard College. After graduating with a degree in 1969, Anderson decided on sculpture as her study for her master at Columbia University, and graduated in 1972.

For a time, Anderson taught art history and Egyptian architecture at the college level, but she was really gearing up to begin professionally as an artist within the year. And not just an artist who presented her work for public consumption in the safety of a gallery, but rather an artist who gave a performance for everyone to view.

As Laurie (not Laura) Anderson, she has a deep desire to communicate something visually, while also wanting to extend beyond the parameters of a structured visual commentary in such things as paintings or sculptures and into the multi-dimensional direction of films, music and the spoken word. With a history of both music and sculpture, it was no surprise to see that Anderson move in that direction.

By the late 1970's, Laurie Anderson had carved out a career for herself as a successful artist. She was also known as a source for the soundtracks of experimental films during that period, so her status in the art society was pretty well established. Yet, she discovered that just as the general public tended to look with disdain at art as being pretentious, those in the art circles were just as closed minded about reaching the general public with their art. It was at that point that Anderson began to format her work towards the everyman instead of just the crowd who was already getting the message.

Having had previous recording experience (she had already recorded one album of poetry by the very early 1980's), she was interested in going further with recording music

and decided to use a snippet of interpretational electronic music from her multi-media, multi-hour presentation UNITED STATES I-IV to be released as a single. The song became known as *O Superman* and was originally recorded as a mail order item (1,000 copies were made). In fact, Anderson was even taking the orders personally as the records sat in her home, ready to be mailed.

The song — a techno-musical track at a time when musical artists were just discovering the capabilities of electronics in music — was a huge hit in Britain. After receiving orders in the tens of thousands, Anderson signed with Warner Brothers, who had already made moves to sign her up to a contract. *O Superman* eventually reached No. 2 on the UK charts and an album released in 1982, based on even more snippets from the UNITED STATES presentation called BIG SCIENCE, reach No. 29. More importantly, with her understanding of the visual medium involved, Anderson was one of the first musical artists to really dive into the music video method for expanding upon the message behind the music. Also, she was interested in the technological aspects of music videos and was willing to try new techniques to see how well they would work in conjunction with her music. In doing so, Anderson was one of the first to show how video could make a point in addition the music, and show something more than just a singer staring into the camera and singing.

Thanks to the *O Superman* single and the video for it, Anderson had gold hit with the album, but she was intent on working with her live presentation, UNITED STATES I-IV, which was finally seen in the US in 1983. She then followed this up in 1984 with her second musical album, MISTER HEARTBREAK, which some consider the most musical of her albums. This album didn't do quite as well as BIG SCIENCE, but she had already made her mark as an interpreter of artistic expressions with technologically inclined musical pieces.

The succeeding years have seen more music albums and tours, but Anderson continues to explore new areas of innovation relating to presentation, including the CD-ROM done for her project, PUPPET MOTEL, which came out in 1995. In doing so, Anderson carries on her attempts to bring more cutting edge art to the mass medium of recording and video.

Selected Studio Albums:

- BIG SCIENCE (Warner Brothers, 1982)
- MISTER HEARTBREAK (Warner Brothers, 1984)
- HOME OF THE BRAVE (Warner Brothers, 1986)
- STRANGE ANGELS (Warner Brothers, 1989)

- ○ BRIGHT RED (Warner Brothers, 1994)
- ○ THE UGLY ONE WITH THE JEWELS (Warner Brothers, 1995)

Live Albums:
- ○ UNITED STATES LIVE (Warner Brothers, 1984)

~ 3 ~
Lavern Baker

Throughout the pages of rock history are many cases of performers who had gained fame and perhaps a little fortune (although that wasn't always the case) with a performing persona that they were stuck with long after its usefulness was gone. In these pages alone there are tales of performers who built a career on being a specific type of performer (from balladeer at one extreme to punk singer at the other), only to see public sentiment shift away, leaving them struggling to find another niche in which to continue their careers.

That wasn't the case with LaVern Baker.

Some found the freedom for their singing or playing through the magic of Rock and Roll.

That wasn't the case with LaVern Baker.

Some left the world of music behind, only to be rediscovered in a later age and given a chance to redeem themselves in the public eye.

That wasn't the case with LaVern Baker.

Heck, that wasn't even her real name.

Born November 11, 1929 in Chicago, Illinois, Baker made a mystery out of her real name (stating only that Baker was her father's name, and that Delores Williams (the name often mentioned as her real name) was a name that she went by for only a short time in her life), leaving historians and the public alike with only the stage name she had used for many years. Her career as a singer started in 1939 at the age of ten after winning a Jitterbug contest and being given a chance to sing for the crowd at a dance hall. After that she began singing at a variety of clubs until, at the age of 17, she was signed to sing at the Club DeLisa in Chicago. Billed for a time as "Little Miss Sharecropper" (a title she hated, especially as she had to complete the illusion by wearing raggedy clothes when on stage), LaVern did well enough to begin recording music by the age of 20 with Eddie "Sugarman" Penigar's band for RCA Victor.

The next few years saw LaVern bouncing around — playing at different clubs and recording under the name of Bea Baker and finally as LaVern Baker — mainly etched into

the pop ballad genre. That is, until 1953, when she was signed with Atlantic Records. At Atlantic, Baker was continuing her much enjoyed role as a torch singer, but she was also hitting it big on the R&B charts with material like *Tweedlee Dee* and *Bop-Ting-A-Ling*. But what really caught LaVern up in the emerging Rock and Roll honor roll was her rocking abilities in songs like *Jim Dandy* coupled with her work with disc jockey Alan Freed. Freed, who would become synonymous with the term "Rock and Roll," had not only been playing her songs on his radio show, but had also invited Baker to perform in shows staged by Freed for the emerging Rock and Roll audience. She also made appearances in two early rock films (which starred Freed as well). In doing so, she provided the few visual references of the early rock days that proved a woman could get along in the new genre — as well as any man could.

And all this was enough to firmly place LaVern Baker into the roll of Rock and Roll diva. But it wasn't something that left her with any great sense of achievement. She was already known through chart hits, and it seemed a little bit odd to suddenly be the darling of a new musical genre, when it seemed to her like a just name change of what she'd already been doing anyway.

Besides, she wanted to be known as a singer of songs — not just the singer of one specific type of music. She didn't want to be pigeonholed, and being played on the Rock and Roll shows and touring with the Rock and Roll cavalcade of stars in the late 1950's and early 1960's did little to abate her feeling of drifting towards a status that would confine her.

Not that she let it worry her. Instead, she continued performing and recording through part of the 1960's (including a rendition of *See See Rider* that's considered definitive in most musical circles), in a variety of musical genres, with no regrets. Then, in the late 1960's, LaVern Baker disappeared.

That is, disappeared from the view of the American public. As it turned out, she had gone to entertain the troops during the Vietnam War and had ended up in a hospital from an enlarged heart and a collapsing lung. After a doctor in Hong Kong prescribed a warmer climate, LaVern's agent suggested the Philippines. From there she played some hotels until she ended up working at the military bases and eventually the Marine Staff NCO Club. Working as the entertainment director of the club, LaVern found not only a healthier climate, but one that allowed her to experiment with any type of music she wished, whenever she wished. Having an audience that changed every night, with an appetite for musical styles that changed every night, LaVern found herself fitting into the mix readily and with no regrets.

In fact, it wasn't until the late 1980's that LaVern found herself in the US again, after people had been clamoring to find out where she disappeared to in 1970. By that time, she hadn't sung her hits in years and had little idea why anyone would want to hear her sing them now. Nevertheless, she came back in 1988 to sing at Atlantic Record's fortieth anniversary party. It was there that she ran into Ruth Brown (see her entry later in the book) who was appearing on Broadway in BLACK AND BLUE, a production featuring many blues hits from over the years. When Brown suggested that Baker take over for her in the show, LaVern at first was reluctant, figuring that her job was at the Club and not back in the US. After two years, however, Baker had been won over (because of the money offered and the continuing political problems in the Philippines) and moved back to the US to work on the show.

With the success of the show, and the renewed interest in blues and the early stages of rock music, Baker reentered the American music scene with tremendous attention. It was enough to see a live album be released in 1991 and a studio album in 1992, not to mention offers to perform live again for American audiences. Which was fine with LaVern Baker, although she had no burning desire to sell hit records or sell out shows.

Her concern rested entirely with being able to sing and have a good time singing for the crowds, whomever they might be. She kept to that way of thinking up until her passing on March 10, 1997. Singing was the goal, and in the end that was exactly what she got.

Selected Studio Albums:
- LAVERN BAKER (Atlantic, 1953)
- LAVERN (Atlantic, 1956)
- SINGS BESSIE SMITH (Atlantic, 1958)
- SAVED (Atlantic, 1959)
- SEE SEE RIDER (Atlantic, 1963)
- WOKE UP THIS MORNIN' (DRG, 1992)
- BLUES SIDE OF ROCK 'N' ROLL (Star Club, 1993)

Best of the "Best Of" Albums:
- THEIR GREATEST HITS (Atlantic, 1953)
- SOUL ON FIRE: THE BEST OF LAVERN BAKER (Rhino, 1991)

Live Albums:
- LAVERN BAKER LIVE IN HOLLYWOOD '91 (Rhino, 1991)

~ 4 ~
Toni Basil

Okay, so why is Toni Basil here? Isn't there only one song to remember?

For some that's probably the case, but that's not the end of the story. Additionally, her achievements with just that one song alone are enough to cement her place as one of the most influential women rockers.

Born in Philadelphia, Pennsylvania in 1950, Basil had taken up dancing at a young age and eventually relocated to California to dance and do choreography. It was there that she began working in films, especially material involving Bob Rafelson. Through the late 1960's and early 1970's, Basil was involved in three films for Bob, appearing in two as an actress (EASY RIDER and FIVE EASY PIECES, both starring Jack Nicholson) and as a choreographer and dancer in the Monkees' movie HEAD.

After these experiences, Basil was increasingly known as valuable a person to use behind the camera and her career was assured. Yet, it wasn't quite enough and in 1981, Basil decided to try her hand at doing a record album. Caught in the middle of the emerging new wave movement, she began forming material for her first album, WORD OF MOUTH. To get started, she recorded a song called *Mickey*, a catchy cheerleader anthem to a boyfriend crush set to a wavering keyboard and clunking drum mix.

At first, nobody was sure if the song would be a hit, but after much interest overseas it was released in the US and became one of those infectious pop songs that took over the country in the early days of the 1980's. But one hit single was not the main reason for Toni's placement in history — it was the promotion done for the single that did the trick.

Not having enough material for a tour, and certainly not wanting to spend time away from other things doing a bunch of promotional live appearances (especially with no band to help support the music), Basil instead created a promotional film for the song. The film, continuing the thread of the cheerleading melody to the extreme, featured Toni in all of her cheerleading glory, singing the song with a group of cheerleaders behind her.

The film, one of the first breakthrough music videos of the emerging MTV scene, became a huge success. While other artists were still considering the possibilities of the video scene, and some even dismissing the phenomena out-of-hand, Toni Basil jumped right in and came away as the first music video queen of Rock and Roll.

Although Basil expanded on this beginning with more videos and a second album in 1983 (TONI BASIL which featured a Top 20's hit *Over My Head*), the peak had already been reached with *Mickey*. From there on, Basil went on to other productions and other musical outlets, and some tried to brush her off as a one hit wonder — a freak of nature that should not be given a second thought. Yet in an era where most performers were more than satisfied with doing performance-oriented promotional films for their singles, Toni Basil was one of the first to see how a song could be expanded beyond the audio concept and into the visual realm.

Selected Studio Albums:
  ◦ WORD OF MOUTH (Chrysalis, 1981)
  ◦ TONI BASIL (Chrysalis, 1983)

Best of the "Best Of" Albums:
  ◦ THE BEST OF TONI BASIL (Razor & Tie, 1994)

~ 5 ~
Pat Benatar

Record companies are in the business of entertainment. The emphasis in that sentence should be on the word "business," and that's important to remember when considering the careers of some artists. More specifically, we can see how sometimes the "business" has absolutely no idea of how to promote a given performer's career. After all, in any business there are usually a few innovators and then a large group of people who climb on board, take a look around, and copy whatever works. Sometimes, this works out and everyone is pleased, Other times, it has destroyed what could have been a brilliant career if taken in another direction, perhaps stalled a career in progress, or even left a performer spending years working to get beyond the persona given them in their early career.

Case in point: Pat Benatar. An engaging singer with a terrific voice who was thrust upon the rock world in the late 1970's as the latest sex kitten in pop music. Didn't matter if that was necessarily the role she wanted, it was the role that the record company believed was best for her. It was a pit that many female rock performers fell into over the years, but Pat's story is one of the few where corporate uncreative ideals couldn't destroy the talent of the performer.

Born Patricia Andrzejewski on January 10, 1953 in Brooklyn, New York, Pat knew by the age of 12 that her singing voice was extraordinary and was already singing solos in the school choir and appearing in singing competitions. With this in mind, she took vocal training for seven years and was set to go to The Julliard School in New York to study Opera when she decided that the type of training involved was not suited for her and walked away from those possibilities.

Instead, Pat married her high-school boyfriend Dennis Benatar and moved to Richmond, Virginia to study voice at the University of Virginia. At first, it was a fine fix after the disappointment with Julliard, but Pat soon became restless and decided to begin her professional career without waiting any longer.

After a short span working as a singing waitress in a Hopewell, Virginia restaurant, Pat hooked up with a band called Coxon's Army in 1974-75. It was a good starting point for her, as the band became well-known in the Virginia area releasing a single (*Day Gig* backed with *Last Saturday*), a self-named album and even going so far as to have their own hour-long special on PBS in the Virginia area. Yet, even then, the lure of a steady gig in a popular band was not enough to satisfy Pat's creative appetite. One major problem was the nature of the band, which leaned toward cover songs, many of which were along Emerson, Lake and Palmer lines. Instead, Pat longed to have a more creative outlet for her vocal talents and saw New York as the place to do it.

Hearing that Catch A Rising Star, a popular New York club which mainly featured comedians, was looking for singers to appear in between the comedy acts, Pat went to New York and almost immediately began working at the club in 1977. It was the true turning point in her career — she became a draw for customers to the club and was later spotted by Chrysalis Records as a possible contender for a record contract.

courtesy Hot Wacks

Signing a deal with the label in 1978, Pat then began working to put a band together and soon recruited Neil Geraldo, who helped her recruit the rest of the band. Time was also needed to decide the direction of the band, with both Pat and Neil wanting to put together a rock album with a variety of material ranging from a touch of hard rock to ballads. The two even began working on material together for the album which was to be produced by Ron Dante.

Then came the first event that showed the two exactly how the label saw them. First off, it wasn't supposed to be a band at all, but a singer doing middle-of-the-road pop material. That was much different from what Pat and Neil had expected it to be and after some frustrating time in the studio with Dante, the change was made to Mike Chapman and Peter Coleman as producers for the first album.

The results was Pat's first solo album, IN THE HEAT OF THE NIGHT, which went to No. 12 in the US, thanks partly to the success of the first single, a remake of the song *Heartbreaker*, which reached No. 23 in the US. The album eventually went Platinum and Chrysalis was more than happy to have Pat return to the studio for a follow-up album in 1980, CRIMES OF PASSION. It was during this period as well that Pat and Dennis Benatar were divorced, although Pat continued to use her former husband's surname for the rest of her career.

CRIMES OF PASSION continued to show Pat's hit-making capacity, with many singles released (including *You Better Run, Hit Me With Your Best Shot, Treat Me Right*), and with what would become a popular standard on album rock radio stations, *Hell is for Children*. CRIMES OF PASSION eventually reached No. 2 on the US charts (stalled in reaching No. 1 by John Lennon's last album, DOUBLE FANTASY), and Pat received her first Grammy Award for Best Female Rock Vocal Performance for the album. The time period of the second album also saw Pat actively dating Neil Geraldo, although the two would break up for a time during the making of the third album, PRECIOUS TIME.

CRIMES OF PASSION was helped by the new MTV cable network which began showing music videos on a 24 hour basis. At that time, the number of performers making videos for their singles was still quite small, but Chrysalis had already produced one for *You Better Run*, and a desperate MTV ran the video constantly lacking a wide selection of other material. It was this repetition that helped *You Better Run* to become such a big hit.

At first, it seemed that the record label wasn't sure how to promote Pat Benatar, especially considering that the first album showed a rough, rock edge to her vocals. It was decided to play up the "tough sexy" angle of their new performer, both in ads and on the record covers. At first, this was just par for the course in the band's eyes, and they were more concerned with putting out good material on their albums. Then Pat saw an ad for the second album that, through the use of airbrushing, made her appear not only topless but with additional cleavage. It was the first real breaking point, and the battle between Pat and the record label began.

PRECIOUS TIME came out in 1981 with somewhat of a departure of the "sexy" look on cover of the album. The album's lyrics showed development as well, with songs centering more on relationships, much like the real life turbulence facing Neil and Pat at the time. The album not only hit No. 1 in the US, but was also their first album to break through the Top 40 in the UK, hitting No. 30. The album also spawned a number of popular singles, including the title track plus *Fire And Ice* (for which Pat won her second Grammy) and *Promises In The Dark*."

Demand for more material lead to the band returning to the studios in 1982, but not before Neil and Pat reconciled and married on February 20, 1982 in Maui. The next album, GET NERVOUS, was released in November 1982. It reached No. 4 in the US and feature even more hit singles, including *Shadows of the Night, Little Too Late* and

Looking For A Stranger. Pat once again won the Best Female Rock Vocals at the Grammy's for *Shadows Of The Night.* Things seemed to be going great for Pat and the band.

But friction between the band and the label was increasing. A hot point was the cover of the GET NERVOUS album — the label less than thrilled with the humorous nature of the cover (of which the final back cover photos was to be the front) and told Pat to have the front cover reshot with her in "attractive" makeup. Pat especially was getting fed up with the image she had to portray and wanted to move outside of it.

Good news came with the release of the live album, LIVE FROM EARTH, which not only hit No. 13 in the US, but had a hit single with *Love is a Battlefield,* which reached No. 5 in the US and led to Pat's fourth straight Grammy award in 1984. However, the band saw little relief and went straight back into the studio in 1984 for the November release of their next album, TROPICO.

It was with TROPICO that fans and the press alike could see that the "sex kitten" role Pat had been cornered into was being lifted away. The cover depicted her in an almost baroque fantasy setting and the songs were more fanciful and enchanting than the harder material on earlier albums. *We Belong,* the first single from the TROPICO reached No. 5 (No. 22 in the UK), while the album itself went to No. 14 in the US. *Ooh Ooh Song* was also be released as a single and hit No. 36, but the next top ten single for Pat wouldn't come until September 1985 with the release of *Invincible* from the LEGEND OF BILLIE JEAN move soundtrack album.

The band had hoped to take a break, but the record company insisted on a new album in 1985. The result was SEVEN THE HARD WAY, which reached No. 26 in the US and featured only two singles. The label was no doubt less than thrilled by the first single, *Sex as a Weapon,* a song dealing with exploitation of sex to sell products, especially in light of the fact that her first two album covers were used in the music video as examples of such exploitation. Of course, some critics, not seeing the irony of the situation, voiced their complaints that Pat was being hypocritical of her own past in doing the song. In doing so, they missed the point entirely. This song was the closing of one door in Pat's career and the opening of another.

After 6 years of constant recording and touring, Pat decided to take some time away from the limelight for her family. So it wasn't until August 1988 that Pat returned with the release of WIDE AWAKE IN DREAMLAND. This album reached No. 28 in the US and No. 11 in the UK, with the first single, *All Fired Up* reaching No. 19 in both the US and the UK. It was a hit for the label, but Pat waited another three years before recording another album. To make up for the empty time, her label released the "greatest hits" package, BEST SHOTS, in 1989.

Her next album was TRUE LOVE, an album that was more blues than rock oriented, and would have sent a chill down Chrysalis' collective spine if they hadn't already been in flux over the company being sold. It was a prime time for Pat, Neil and the band to walk as well, given that their contract had reached a point where they could move on if they wanted to. Instead, Chrysalis okayed the recording and release of the album, thereby allowing Pat to move into other musical genres of her own free will instead of being pushed into certain directions by an quasi-autocratic record label.

1993 saw the release of another album, GRAVITY'S RAINBOW, the last album under contract with Chrysalis. It was followed in 1997 with INAMORATA, with total creative control going to Pat and Neil. 1999 was the 20th anniversary of Pat's first solo album and it was celebrated with the release of the three-CD anthology album, SYNCHRONISTIC WANDERINGS. Talk continues regarding a new studio album as well.

Twenty years have passed. In many cases, the span of a pop star's career is a couple of albums, if they're lucky. In the case of Pat Benatar, it was in small part luck, but mostly a huge amount of talent and a lot of guts that got her through those years — not only as an artist, but also as a hit maker in a world dominated by singers with careers that live and die with the passing fancies of the public and the record labels. It took a while and it took being somewhat subversive as well, but Pat beat the odds and ended up with her own voice not only being her greatest talent, but her direction as well.

Selected Studio Albums:
- IN THE HEAT OF THE NIGHT (Chrysalis, 1979)
- CRIMES OF PASSION (Chrysalis, 1980)
- PRECIOUS TIME (Chrysalis, 1981)
- GET NERVOUS (Chrysalis, 1982)
- TROPICO (Chrysalis, 1984)
- SEVEN THE HARD WAY (Chrysalis, 1985)
- WIDE AWAKE IN DREAMLAND (Chrysalis, 1988)
- TRUE LOVE (Chrysalis, 1991)
- GRAVITY'S RAINBOW (Chrysalis, 1993)
- INNAMORATA (CMC, 1997)

Studio Album (as part of Coxon's Army):
- COXON'S ARMY

Live Albums:
- ○ LIVE FROM EARTH (Chrysalis, 1984)
- ○ 8-15-80 (CMC, 1998)

Best of the "Best Of" Albums:
- ○ BEST SHOTS (Chrysalis, 1989)
- ○ ALL FIRED UP: THE BEST OF PAT BENATAR (Chrysalis, 1994)

Boxed-Set:
- ○ SYNCHRONISTIC WANDERINGS: RECORDED ANTHOLOGY (EMD/Chrysalis, 1999)

~ 6 ~
Bjork

Bjork was a musical prodigy —

No, that's not a good way to describe her, although it's easy to see why so many writers have described that way that over the years. Born November 21, 1965 in Reykjavik, Iceland, by the age of 12 Bjork had seen the release of her first album, BJORK. The album had come about because a recording made by her teachers at Barnamusikskoli Reykjavikur (the music school she entered at age 5 and graduated from at 15) that was heard on the national radio service, Radio 1, in Iceland and was a huge success. So was the album, going Platinum. Just think, a Platinum Album at age 12.

But the album was made up of several cover songs (translated into Icelandic) and recorded with many top musicians in the country. Bjork was the singer, not the producer or sole composer. Of course, there was still the impressive fact that an 11 year old was singing on the entire album, and she did write some of her own material. More than enough reasons to be impressed. Yet, to use the word prodigy brings up images of the young performer who burns out early and dies penniless and insane. Instead, Bjork was seemingly less than thrilled with the fame and fortune that the album brought and instead turned her back on it for a time to concentrate on playing music for her own enjoyment and not for claims of success. Besides, with a population well under 300,000, an album could go Platinum at 7,000 copies.

So, scratch prodigy off the list. Going a bit further into her career, Bjork had returned to performing with the breakout of the punk movement while still in her teens. But one can't exactly say that she was a forerunner in the punk movement. Her early collaborative efforts with other musicians went from an all girl punk band in 1979 (called Spit and Snot), to a jazz-fusion group called Exodus, to a one-gig new wave experiment called Jam 80. As things stood, it wasn't until late 1981 that Bjork found some label success with a band, this one called Tappi Tikarrass (which translates as "cork the bitch's ass"). Between 1981 and 1983, Tappi Tikarrass recorded two albums and had some success, but the band members had burnt out and the group disbanded in 1983. Bjork moved on to singing and playing keyboards for a cover band called Cactus during the next two years.

So, Bjork had a failed career, right? No, that doesn't work, because at the same time that she was singing in a cover band, she had joined a recurring lineup in a band called Kukl (which translates as either sorcery or witchcraft). Taking a cue from Siouxsie and the Banshees, the band was a mixture of punk and what was to become known at Goth — a dark lyrical dance music that became tremendously popular in the mid- to late-1980's. Kukl recorded two albums and received enough success for the albums to be released outside of Iceland.

So Bjork was a leader in the Goth movement? Well, you certainly could say that she was in a band that displayed the roots of the Goth movement, perhaps even say that she had continued this style in her later music as well. Yet, it was only two albums over a three year period, for Kukl broke up in 1986 in order to transform into the band that is probably best known of her groups before her solo success in the 1990 — The Sugarcubes.

Including three former members of Kukl, including Thor Eldon Johnson (whom Bjork would marry and have a son with in 1986), The Sugarcubes were the band that obtained the first real international success for Bjork and her compatriots. Writing songs made up of quirky (yet catchy) pop sounds, mixed with a dance beat, a dash of punk and a skewed way of lyric writings that could have only come from a foreign source, The Sugarcubes recorded three albums between 1986 and 1992. Getting a deal with Elektra in the US, The Sugarcubes became known on the growing alternative rock music scene and on radio stations that were beginning to experiment with playing alternative music outside the world of college dormitories.

So, was Bjork's career like that of other famous women singers, who started in one band and then sought success outside of that band? Well, yes and no. After all, Bjork did have one solo album release in 1990, made up of jazz standards. And let's not forget her earlier work in other bands and her first solo album when she was 12. Yet, going solo was probably not that far off the map. After divorcing Johnson in 1989, the band began to drift somewhat and by 1992 — as with so many other projects before it — the musicians had decided to break up and move on to other things.

For Bjork, this meant a solo album and a change in scenery. Moving to London, England, Bjork completed her first international solo album, DEBUT, which was released to great success in many parts of the world. That album in some ways continued elements left over from The Sugarcubes — the manic lyrics and the excessive dance-beat — but there was also a stranger, perhaps darker tone to the music as well. Bjork's singing was also becoming more aggressive, switching from soft lullaby whispers to high-pitched shrieking in only a couple of bars within a song. The lyrics were becoming a bit more introspective and poetic as well.

So, Bjork's story is one of an artist who struggled in bands only to become an international success once she moved to London and went solo. The end.

Well, that doesn't quite cut it either. 1994 turned out to be a major promotional year for Bjork, as she still found time to record a follow-up album, POST, which was released that same year. 1994 and 1995 had Bjork making major appearances in Europe and the US, both on television and in concert (including an MTV special), but the strain of promotion and of London was beginning to take its toll on her (including a much-publicized physical attack of a TV reporter in February 1996). Thus, in 1997 she moved to Spain and began work on her next album, HOMOGENIC.

While HOMOGENIC was another step down the darker road of the lyrics from Bjork's earlier albums, it was obvious that she wasn't interested in simply retreading her past musical accomplishments into another product. Moreover, there was a definite look towards her homeland in some of the lyrics, and in 1998 she returned to Iceland.

So Bjork returned home and started putting together the pieces of her past. Right?

Well, there were no pieces to put together. Things were fine at home. She just returned to Iceland and continues working on different musical projects, including a movie musical completed in 1999 and her follow-up to HOMOGENIC — a follow-up that she's said will go in a different direction than the album before it.

No. Using easy cliches about Bjork just doesn't work. There's neither tragic story here, nor abrupt changes. Instead, it's really a story about a person whose career has been based on a need to create music. It doesn't have to be rock music or some "alternative" take on the music scene at large. There's no mindset that seems concerned about what the latest trend is and how to market it to make money. There's just a person who's lived a life of music and has let it take her wherever she needed to go to fulfill that life. In doing what she wanted in music, her music has influenced others towords attempting a variety of styles without restrictions.

A free spirit of music. Perhaps fitting in the spirit world of her music.

Selected Studio Albums:
- ○ BJORK (Falkinn, 1977)
- ○ DEBUT (Elektra, 1993)
- ○ POST (Elektra, 1995)
- ○ HOMOGENIC (Elektra, 1997

Studio Albums (as part of Tappi Tikarrass):
- ○ BITIO FAST I VITIO (SPOR, 1982)
- ○ MIRANDA (Gramm, 1983)

Studio Albums (as part of Kukl):
- ○ THE EYE (Crass Records, 1984)

Studio Albums (as part of The Sugarcubes):
- ○ LIFE'S TOO GOOD (Elektra, 1988)
- ○ HERE TODAY, TOMORROW NEXT WEEK! (Elektra, 1989)
- ○ IT'S IT (Elektra, 1992)

~ 7 ~
Ruth Brown

A common occurrence in rock music histories is writers who look at how rock was created with a fusion of country (some would even say a dash of bluegrass in there as well) and rhythm and blues. Nothing really wrong with that concept since it brings up the images of the outsiders from the conventional Top 10 Hit Parade that the country's elders were listening to in the early 1950's. A problem does arise, however, when writers focus on the male artists that changed the course of music with the creation of rock music and giving little room to the women that were there as well.

When they do this, women performers who specialized in top tempo jazz and rhythm and blues tend to get overlooked, briefly mention if acknowledged at all. This abandonment isn't really the intention of these authors, but rather a sense of wanting to get on with the story and stress the importance of the many male artists who formed rock music. But this does the reader a terrible disservice.

Ruth Brown (along with LaVern Baker and Etta James, among others) is one of the performers from the early days of the transition from R&B and Country to the rock sound of the late 1950's and 1960's. Although the majority of her material would be commonly classified as R&B or even blues, her music had a hip sound to it that was a key element of the rockabilly sound of the latter 1950's.

Born Ruth West on January 12, 1928, Ruth truly began her singing career by sneaking behind her father's back to perform with the local USO. When disapproval from her father became too great, Ruth set out on her own at the age of 16 and soon met up with the man she would marry, trumpeter Jimmy Brown. Although the two would work together for some time, Ruth (who now went by her married name) ended up performing on her own by 1947 and ended up working for Cab Calloway's sister Blanche Calloway at their nightclub, the Crystal Caverns.

A horrible auto accident left Ruth unable to perform for several months and saw her marriage to Jimmy Brown end, but by mid-1949 she had become noticed by the record labels and signed to Atlantic. By 1953, she had gone on to have hit after hit for Atlantic, so much so that Atlantic Records would become known as "the house that Ruth built." Her vocal stylings were an excellent mix with songs that had traces of an early Rock and Roll beat, mainly material like *(Mama) He Treats Your Daughter Mean* and *5-10-15 Hours*. Her music was also an early establishment of the "good girl gone bad" image that has served so many women rockers over the years (in fact she recorded a song called *Help a Good Girl Go Bad*) during this part of her career.

As the 1960's came, however, the interests of the label and the public alike turned to music that was directed towards the growing Soul and Rock movement, with Soul leaning towards a dance movement that would become a standard for the industry by the late 1960's. Ruth Brown's career ended up stalling during those years, and while the late 1970's were a bit kinder, it wasn't really until the 1980's that her career was rejuvenated.

A return to the good graces of the labels, thanks in part to her work in the Broadway production, BLACK AND BLUE, didn't change Ruth's tune about what had happened to her during the lean years in between. Using her fame to her advantage, Ruth was one of the early members of a group of people working for royalty payments to early performers of the R&B and rock years that had been misdirected in contractual agreements, or who had just never were paid what was owed to them. This came about after a nine year struggle with Atlantic to get royalties due to her, and after seeing how hard it was for someone to get anything out of a major label, she was sure that there were many less fortunate that needed that chance as well. Thus, she helped found the Rhythm & Blues Foundation in help other performers get royalties due them.

In a career that reached a zenith in the 1950's, then peaked again in the 1980's and 90's, Ruth Brown was an originator in the rock movement because of her singing style, but she was more than that with her return. Although she still blesses us all with her singing, she continues to bless those who have been left along the wayside by the record labels with her continuing work for securing artists' royalties. That only makes the originator even more of a one-of-a-kind.

Selected Studio Albums:
- RUTH BROWN SINGS FAVORTIES (Atlantic, 1956)
- LATE DATE WITH RUTH BROWN (Atlantic, 1956)
- RUTH BROWN (Atlantic, 1957)
- ALONG COMES RUTH (Philips, 1962)
- GOSPEL TIME (Polygram, 1962)
- HELP A GOOD GIRL GO BAD (DCC, 1963)
- RUTH BROWN '65 (Mainstream, 1964)
- FINE BROWN FRAME (Capitol, 1968)
- BLACK IS BROWN AND BROWN IS BEAUTIFUL (DCC, 1969)
- TAKIN' CARE OF BUSINESS (Stockholm, 1980)
- BLUES ON BROADWAY (Fantasy, 1989)
- BROWN, BLACK & BEAUTIFUL (Ichiban, 1990)
- FINE AND MELLOW (Fantasy, 1991)
- THE SONGS OF MY LIFE (Fantasy, 1993)
- R+B = RUTH BROWN (Bullseye Blues, 1997)
- GOOD DAY FOR THE BLUES (Bullseye Blues, 1999)

Live Albums:
- HAVE A GOOD TIME (Fantasy, 1988)
- LIVE IN LONDON (Jazz House Records, 1996)

Best of the "Best Of" Albums:
- MISS RHYTHM (GREATEST HITS AND MORE) (Rhino — reissue, 1949)
- THE BEST OF RUTH BROWN (Rhino — reissue, 1949)
- THE BEST OF RUTH BROWN (Atlantic, 1963)

~ 8 ~
Kate Bush

"Let me in your window . . ."

Perhaps a warning label should be placed on all of Kate Bush's albums that state "Abandon hope all ye that enter here!" There seems to be some danger to the psyche whenever someone takes his or her first steps into Kate's musical realm and people seem to instantly either love her work completely or despise it with a passion. Combine that with the mystery of a performer who has has released new material only when she feels it's ready, taking little heed of record label and fan alike when they're eager, almost desperate to hear something new from her. She's a performer who seems to put so much passion into her work yet seems strikingly distant in interviews; a performer who is considered highly influential to many other artists and has a huge following in most parts of the world, yet is little known in the US beyond a cult following.

A mystery. And everyone loves a mystery.

"Let me steal this moment from you."

Born Catherine Bush on July 30, 1958, Kate began playing music at an early age as part of her education. At the age of 12 she took up the piano and at 13 began her first attempts to put some of her poems to music. In 1972, a friend of the family, Ricky Hopper, thought enough of Kate's work that he tried to place some of her songs for possible use with other artists through several record labels. When Kate's demos were rejected, Hopper got into contact with an old acquaintance from Cambridge University, David Gilmour, a member of the rock band Pink Floyd.

As luck would have it, Gilmour was looking for other artists to work with and perhaps assist in launching their careers. Liking the material he heard, Gilmour had Kate record new demos in 1973 with him and a few fellow musicians. However, no interest came from the record labels with these demos either. Feeling frustrated at the lack of interest, Gilmour worked with Kate to produce a three-track professional level demo tape, which he then passed on to Bob Mercer at EMI. EMI's General Manager liked what he heard and started working on putting together a deal for Kate.

By July 1976, barely 18 years old, Kate had signed a deal with EMI. While some record labels may have used her youth to their advantage, many reports suggest that EMI was willing to let her work on her material and sharpen her skills before recording her first album. With the money that came in signing the contract, along with a small inheritance, Kate spent the first year of her contract working on demos. She also took time to study dance and perform in a cover band called the KT Bush Band between April and June 1976 with Del Palmer, Brian Bath, Charlie Morgan and her brother, Paddy.

"But they told us all they wanted was a sound that could kill someone . . ."

Although EMI seemed paternal, by August 1977 the label was anxious to get Kate into a studio and begin recording material, since it had been a year since she'd been signed. The album was completed by September 1977 and EMI was gearing up to release a track called *James and the Cold Gun* as the first single. Some, however, felt that *Wuthering Heights* would make a better single, including Kate, who was also reportedly not thrilled with the cover photo planned for the single. By the time things were settled it was already November and EMI was unsure if it was a good idea to push their new artist during the turbulent Christmas holiday season. It was decided instead to hold off the release of the single until January 1978.

That decision didn't stop a few promos from hitting the radio airwaves, however, and the single was on the air consistently during the holiday season. Because of this, when the single finally hit the commercial marketplace, it took off. It reached No. 1 in the UK within six weeks of its commercial debut and held the top spot for four weeks. Her first album, THE KICK INSIDE, was released during the middle of all the hoopla in February 1978 and reached a high of No. 3 on the charts by April. The second single in the UK was determined by Kate and *The Man With the Child in His Eyes* was released in May 1978, while *Them Heavy People* was released as the second single in most other parts of the world.

By mid-1978, Kate had become one of the best selling female artists in the UK. Her single *Wuthering Heights* had also hit No. 1 in many countries around the world. Yet, in the US, where the first album was released twice because of changes in distribution by EMI, THE KICK INSIDE received very little notice except on some college radio stations. As for why that was — well, it probably had much to do with the state of the music scene in the US during 1978, a period when the audience was split between soft pop, heavy disco, and the deafening roar of punk. The experimental stages that would help boost the new wave movement in the US were still about two years away. In essence, Kate's music was about two years ahead of its time. And besides, promoters probably just saw the pictures and figured the album for another one-hit-wonder from a pretty little girl and nothing more, never even giving the music a chance to speak for itself.

After a while, Kate started picking up a following in the US. Yet, it was an audience made up of college students who were looking for something a bit different, perhaps even experimental. Her music also became immensely popular among fantasy, comic book and science fiction fans, especially after the release of her second album LIONHEART, which featured a homage to the horror movie studio, Hammer, in the song *Hammer Horror* (the ghost story basis of *Wuthering Heights* didn't hurt either). Otherwise, it was a thin crossover market, leaving Kate without notable success in the US until the release of *Running up That Hill* in 1986 (and even then, it was a minor success compared to her popularity in other parts of the world). She did do some promotion in the US, including an appearance on the NBC TV's SATURDAY NIGHT LIVE in December 1978, but none of it did anything to increase her popularity in the states.

Not that it mattered much really, since everywhere else Kate had a popularity that lead directly to EMI wanting a second album out before Christmas 1978. That second album was LIONHEART and April 1979 was the beginning of the only concert tour of Kate's solo career. Ever. Six weeks of shows and never again. For those who saw it, it was an exceptional show, with Kate on stage for most of the show's 2½ hours. A theatrical show with props, dancing and of course the vocal acrobatics of Kate's voice, which no doubt won over many crowds and was successful enough to generate both a four track EP called KATE BUSH LIVE ON STAGE in September 1979 and, later, the video LIVE AT THE HAMMERSMITH ODEON in 1981.

December 1979 saw Kate doing her own BBC television special, followed by her going back into the studios in January 1980 to work on her third album, NEVER FOR EVER. In January she was also named Best Female Artist in a poll by Record Mirror and Best Female Singer in a poll by New Musical Express, while February found her named Top Female Artist by Music Week and Top Female Singer at the British Rock and Pop Awards. The awards continued to come in the months and years that followed.

"She gotta dance, she gotta dance ..."

NEVER FOR EVER was released in early September 1980 and within a week was at No. 1 on the British album charts — a first for a British solo female artist. Kate worked to promote the album and the many singles from it, but her attention came quickly to focus on the genesis of an album that many fans consider to be one of the peaks in her career, THE DREAMING. The first song from the new album was *Sat In Your Lap*, a major track for the album and one that was released as a single nearly one year and three months before the album hit the marketplace. This was the start of Kate's insistence on working on material until she felt it was ready, leading to more and more time in-between albums as she perfected each song.

The time spent was to good effect, as even though some fans and critics were mystified by the poetic and challenging nature of THE DREAMING, it was another success for Kate in most parts of the world. It also led to a little bit more of a penetration of the US, with several good reviews and an increase in airplay of her work on college radio stations. For the first time, one of Kate's albums had hit the Billboard Top 200 charts, and it was enough to convince EMI to release both LIONHEART and NEVER FOR EVER domestically in the US for the first time. It was really still a small breakthrough, since college radio stations were notorious for being powerful enough to be heard on campus and rarely anywhere else. Nevertheless, it showed that musical preferences in the US were beginning to come in line with Kate's musical direction.

Kate spent most of the next year promoting THE DREAMING, although some of the singles were considered controversial and were rarely heard on the radio in some countries, including the UK. In fact, one single, *There Goes a Tenner*, had such weak promotion and airplay that it didn't even enter the charts officially, the only Kate Bush single not to do so. Not looking back, however, Kate had construction begin on her own studio to record her next album. June 1984 saw her finish the major part of her next album, HOUNDS OF LOVE, only to spend the following year perfecting the overdubs for the music in her private studio. So, nearly three years had passed since her last album when HOUNDS OF LOVE appeared in June 1985. But it was one of her biggest successes, especially in the US.

A video shown on MTV helped to promote the first single from the album, *Running Up That Hill*, and the song was Kate's first single to break through the Top 40 on the Billboard charts, peaking at No. 30 (which was also the Billboard peak for the album). The album was a critical success as well, and there were certainly no indications that the time Kate spent on the album was a loss by any means. In fact, its success would lead directly to the November 1986 release of THE WHOLE STORY, a compilation album backed with a video compilation, within the year.

Four years passed between studio albums, although Kate undertook many different projects outside of working on her next album, many of these in support of charitable causes. October 1989 saw the release of THE SENSUAL WORLD. It reached No. 43 in the US and No. 2 in the UK, but problems with promotion led to weaker interest in the album and its singles than with Kate's earlier albums. Columbia, her label in the US, was unsure of how to promote the album, especially in light of the growing alternative / grunge movement occurring within the country. Meanwhile,

Kate herself had backed off on the amount of promotion that she did in relation to her earlier albums, and it left some of the normal outlets (radio and record stores) somewhat cool to the idea of promoting an album that the label wasn't. There were also complaints by some fans of poor sound quality on the album. Still, there remains little to suggest that the album's weaker sales numbers were little more than just a one-off situation. Especially considering that the following year saw the release of a huge boxed-set called THIS WOMAN'S WORK.

"My goal is moving near . . ."

Four more years passed between studio albums, with THE RED SHOES being released in 1993. This album hit No. 28 in the US, a new album peak for Kate, and No. 2 in the UK. THE RED SHOES also led to the release of a 43-minute film, directed by Kate, called THE LINE, THE CROSS, AND THE CURVE in 1994. It was the last full solo project that Kate released in the 1990's.

Since then, there have been rumblings in fan circles about Kate Bush, her projects and when a new album will be released. As each year stretches into the next, the rumors grow and the anticipation of the fans is dimmed, as people realize that the rumors are only that. While talk does continue that Kate is working on new material, she has made enough appearances on other albums to help take the edge off of the fan's anticipation.

"I just know that something good is going to happen. And I don't know when, but just saying it could even make it happen."

So, over a twenty year career there have been seven studio albums, a boxed-set and a few live and compilations albums. Some may look at this and suggest that it's not a healthy output for an artist. However, the idea that performers have to release new material on a more regular basis often leads to sacrificing the integrity of the music for the sake of the purse strings. Kate's work is not done along those lines and the repeated success of her music after long and careful refinement proves that there's certainly nothing wrong in working to produce the best.

Even more, her careful structuring of the music to her poetic lyrics have made Kate one of the main female songwriters of the 1970's and 1980's and helped lay the groundwork for the growing number of women songwriters who are now experimenting in their work. Although some attempts in today's pop world are half-hearted, there are many performers, such as Bjork and Tori Amos, who have acknowledged that Kate's work propelled their own music onward. There was also the ability of Kate's songwriting to suggest that not every song done by a solo female artist had to be either a love song or some type of novelty act. There could be strong messages about relationships, war, fantasy, sex and even love, explored in the music as well.

In response to the work of songwriter / performers such as Kate Bush, Patti Smith, Stevie Nicks and Siouxsie Sioux, among others, the world has had to adjust its collective ears and temperament somewhat, but have done so without too much in the way of growing pains. The work of these ladies has helped to form a conscious ability of the listening public to hear what is being said and understand that sometimes a female singer may have something to say.

But all of this is the public importance of Kate's work. There's still the mystery of what drives her to do the music that she does. There's the mystery as to why it took so long for the public in the US to catch on.

Most importantly, there is this uncanny ability of her music to stick in your mind and for the words continue to merge in and out of consciousness until the inner thoughts of her message become clear. It's a revelation that may explain the mystery of why Kate has so many followers today.

And every day a new convert.

"All yours, Babooshka, Babooshka, Babooshka!"

Selected Studio Albums:
- THE KICK INSIDE (EMI, 1978)
- LIONHEART (EMI, 1978)
- NEVER FOR EVER (EMI, 1980)
- THE DREAMING (EMI, 1982)
- HOUDS OF LOVE (EMI, 1985)
- THE SENSUAL WORLD (EMI, 1989)
- THE RED SHOES (EMI, 1993)

Live Albums:
- LIVE AT THE HAMMERSMITH ODEON (EMI, 1994 — reissue of the video-cassette from Kate's 1979 only tour came with a CD of the live material from the video as well).

Best of the "Best Of" Albums:
- THE WHOLE STORY (EMI, 1986)

Boxed-Sets:
- THE SINGLE FILE (EMI, 1984 — boxed-set of all UK 7" singles up through 1984)
- THIS WOMAN'S WORK (EMI, 1990, boxed-set of all previous studio albums plus two additional Discs of B-sides, etc.).

~ 9 ~
Karen Carpenter

One thing that can be seen looking at the history of so many performers is that image, or rather "Image" (with a capital "I") has done much to push many performers into stardom. It can also trap them just as easily, whether it's the public's perception of what the person can do, or the Industry's evaluation of a performer's ability.

Karen Carpenter faced that dilemma, and even nearly twenty years after her death, the public's perception of her image is still the one that that hung over her during her life. She's remembered as the sweet voiced singer of The Carpenters, a duo who produced melodious love songs, with little bite, that became popular because they were safe, homogenous songs of little warmth. That image, of course, is completely the work of people who knew nothing of The Carpenters and nothing of Karen. Nevertheless it's an image that will be forever remembered when Karen's name is thought of.

It's a shame, because there's so much more to remember.

Born March 2, 1950, Karen grew up with music all around her thanks to her father's record collection which both she and her brother Richard listened to. The albums enticed Richard to seriously take up music and when Karen had seen how much fun Richard seemed to be having with his studies, she wanted to try her hand as well. When a first attempt at the flute went nowhere, Karen instead tried the drums. Although many people, including family members, felt that drums were not an instrument suitable to a girl, Karen took to the drums immediately and became accomplished enough to join Richard in a band called the Richard Carpenter Trio in 1964. That band eventually recorded one single in 1966, by which time they had realized that Karen had a natural singing voice — a voice which struck people as one of the best elements of the group.

It was Karen's voice that became the focus of her career from that point forward. Although she never gave up the drums, and sometimes played them in concert, the image of Karen Carpenter, the singer, was already being molded into one that everyone — fans and non-fans alike — would remember. Yet, Karen was a unique musical talent: a women drummer who sang most of the group's songs. Sure, there had been other bands and singing groups that had featured drummers who sang lead vocals, and there had certainly been bands (mostly all-female bands) that had featured a women drummer, but Karen was an example of a woman drummer who sang. She was certainly the only one that sang nearly all of the group's material.

It was this image of Karen at the drums that lead to others rethinking their views about drums as an instrument for girls. After all, Karen Carpenter was the pinnacle of the sweet voiced singers, and here she was manning the masculine power of the drums. And it couldn't be passed off in the usual way by thinking that it was an all girl band anyway, so the drummer had to be a woman, because that wasn't the case. Karen was playing the drums because she wanted to, not because she had to. It was a startling image, and it shook some people up. It made them think, however, that maybe other women could go in that direction and it was an image that shaped the musical world for the better.

In 1969, Karen and Richard had become a duo and had recorded a demo tape that ended up in the hands of musician Herb Albert. Albert, who co-owned A&M Records, thought that there was much promise in the duo and signed them up to A&M. By November 1969, the first Carpenters album, OFFERING, was released. The first single off of the album didn't make the Top 40, which was understandable for a first album. But the second single, *Close to You* was a smash surprise hit, reaching No. 1 in just under six weeks.

With that one single, the Carpenters began to dominate the pop music world — with 17 Top 20 hits in the US alone. They toured extensively throughout the 1970's as well, often to capacity crowds.

Yet, there was growing trouble inside the wall of success. The Carpenters were perceived as a cotton candy type confection by many rock fans and by musicians as well. There was a tendency to perceive the Carpenters as similar to the Brady Bunch or the Partridge Family — something nice and sweet for people who didn't want to listen to real rock music anymore. Something safe. And, although Richard knew that the perception was there and that there was little he could do about changing it, the problem bothered Karen considerably more.

When Richard announced to Karen that he was taking some time off in 1979, she decided that this was her chance to work on a solo project. Working with Phil Ramone, Karen began creating an album of more mainstream material with a bit more of an edge to it than what the Carpenters had been doing.

The reaction to this material, once it was recorded, was mixed. For many of the musicians who worked on the project, it was an unveiling of a rock singer that they would never have guessed at before they began working with her. For Richard and others at the record company, it was the most embarrassing and career damaging thing Karen could do. When the time came for the album to be released, the perceived image of what the record would mean to Karen's career — or better yet, what it would mean to The Carpenters' career — led to the decision to put the album on the shelf (and hopefully for good). While the 1983 release of the album VOICE OF THE HEART featured some of Karen's solo recordings, it wasn't until 1996 that the full album finally saw the light of day.

Brother and sister got back together and began recording, but there were other problems occurring within the group. The interest in The Carpenters was starting to wane. Although they had another hit in the early 1980's, the crowds were becoming less interested and the hits were not as forthcoming as they had been.

More importantly, Karen suffering more and more from the spiraling effects of anorexia, which had taken a toll on her body by the early 1980's, resulting in several trips to the hospital and concern by those around her that she wouldn't survive much longer. On February 4, 1983, Karen shaped her own final image, one that still persists today: she passed away from massive heart failure — a direct result of anorexia nervosa. Karen's death was much publicized and with it the world began to take notice of the seriousness of anorexia — basically an illness that leads to people to slowly starve themselves to death in order to become thinner. At the time, not many people even knew that such a disorder existed and even fewer talked about it. In the nearly twenty years since, the symptoms have become generally recognized and there is help available to try and bring sufferers back from the brink of disaster.

Unfortunately for Karen, that wasn't the case in the early 1980's. The root cause of her anorexia is not easily determined, and normally in cases like this it isn't a single problem causing all of the symptoms. Some would say that Karen wished to have control over her life instead of living continuously under the shadow of The Carpenters and found that control through her eating habits. Some might say that it was the direct result of a social environment wherein thin women were perceived as successful. And, of course, others would attribute it to many other things. No matter. In the end, it was Karen's image of herself that lead to her suffering — her preconceived image that she needed to be thinner.

It was the Image that mattered — it was the Image that destroyed her.

Studio Albums (as part of The Carpenters):
- OFFERING (A&M, 1969)
- TICKET TO RIDE (A&M, 1970)
- CLOSE TO YOU (A&M, 1970)
- A SONG FOR YOU (A&M, 1972)
- HORIZON (A&M, 1975)
- A KIND OF HUSH (A&M 1976)
- PASSAGE (A&M, 1977)
- CHRISTMAS PORTRAIT (A&M, 1978)
- MADE IN AMERICA (A&M, 1981)
- VOICE OF THE HEART (A&M 1983)
- LOVELINES (A&M, 1989)

Best of the "Best Of" Albums:
- YESTERDAY ONCE MORE (A&M, 1984-85)
- INTERPRETATIONS (A&M, 1995)

Boxed-Set:
- FROM THE TOP (A&M, 1991)

Studio album (as a solo artist):
- KAREN CARPENTER (A&M, 1996, recorded 1979)

~ 10 ~
Cher

The jokes. Good golly, the jokes.

Let's face it, no matter what opinions of Cher are circulating, no matter whether or not you enjoy her music or her acting, no matter if you've never even heard of her before, you're bound to have heard the jokes. The age jokes, the cosmetic surgery jokes, the sappy song jokes. Yeah, yeah, blah, blah. Cher herself has related in interviews how she was sitting in a theater and when her name appeared in the movie trailer for SILKWOOD she heard the snickering and laughter.

It's easy. Way too easy. Because Cher's had a life that's probably been far more public than she would have liked, it's easy to make fun of her — but doing so is a definite disservice. With all that she'shas done, Cher ultimately ended up pushing the envelope for all female performers who've came after her. By accepting the jokes, she's lessened the abuse for those others as well.

Born May 20, 1946 in El Centro, California, Cherilyn Sarkasian La Piere moved to Los Angeles in the early 1960's to learn acting. While in LA, she met and started dating Sonny Bono, who was working for Phil Spector at the time. Sonny tried getting Spector interested in using Cher in the studio, and he agreed, using Cher as a minder for Ronnie Spector and as a backup singer on some of the singles being produced. Following an ill-conceived Beatles tribute called *Ringo, I Love You* (that credited the singing to Bonnie Jo Mason), Sonny suspected that nothing worthwhile was ever going to happen for either of them under Spector's rule.

Instead, Sonny undertook to produce Cher himself, first under the name of Cherilyn, and then the two of them as the duo Caesar and Cleo. Not much happened to Caesar and Cleo, but as Sonny and Cher they were able to sign a deal with Reprise Records and released their first single, *Baby Don't Go*. The single did well locally (in Los Angeles) and that was enough to get them signed with Atlantic Records as part of the Atco label.

While it's tempting to say that Cher's career was based solely on Sonny & Cher, that wasn't actually the case. Sonny still saw potential in Cher's solo career and continued to produced singles for her while they also worked as a duet. Their single for *Just You* did well on the charts in 1965, but it was their next single in August 1965, *I've Got You Babe*, that provided their undeniable breakthrough into the pop world. The song was a No. 1 smash. It was followed in April 1966 with a solo single by Cher (written by Sonny) called *Bang Bang (My Baby Shot Me Down)*. For a time it looked like they were on their way to a standard success story.

But that wasn't to be the case. The jokes soon started coming. Here it was in the late 1960's and although Sonny and Cher looked the part of the hip generation, they didn't really act the part. Nor did they really bother trying beyond the clothing and phrases of the generation. If you look back at the two of them, it's understandable why this was the case. Sonny was already in his mid-30's by the late 1960's and had no interest in a lot of the experimentation that was at the core of the youth movement. Meanwhile, Cher had looked upon Sonny as her protecting husband and felt that if it was good enough for Sonny to avoid things, then it was good enough for her. Because of that sentiment, the twosome were branded as being unhip at a time where everyone was desperate to be hip. Multiply that with the songs Sonny began writing that dealt with such "unhip" topics as divorce and pregnancies — at a time when songs about war and freedom were what people wanted — and it was no wonder that the jokes began. Following their attempt to move into movies with their film GOOD TIMES (which seems almost like a variation of the Monkees movie HEAD combined with the genesis of their 1970's variety show) and Cher's solo attempt with CHASTITY, interest in Sonny and Cher began fading.

By the beginning of the 1970's, Sonny and Cher were reduced to opening for Pat Boone in Las Vegas. It was a sad experience for the duo, but neither was quite ready to let the jokes wash over them and take them to sea. Instead, it was decided to turn those same jokes around to their advantage. Working together they turned their act into not just another Rock and Roll concert, but one that was like an inverted Burns and Allen routine with rock music backing the comedy up (and the husband as the dumb one). Amazingly, it worked. Spotted by the CBS television network, they were given a chance to do their own variety special. When the show did well, Sonny and Cher were given the go-ahead for a regular variety series. For the next three years the twosome would enter the family home and entertainment with jokes made at Sonny's expense and hear Cher sing an assortment of songs from the current pop charts, her own singles, and songs from the past.

For a time it looked as though Sonny and Cher had found their niche in the public eye. But that changed in 1974 when they separated and divorced. For a time, it was assumed that Sonny would be the one to progress immediately on to better things — in consideration of his production background and his drive to make the television series a success — but that wasn't the case. Instead, Cher signed a deal with Warner Brothers for $2.5 million and by February 1975 she was back on the air with her own solo variety series called, simply, CHER.

It was at this time that the other jokes really began. Not only was Cher considered unhip because she was doing a variety series for "the man," but she became involved in a stormy relationship with Gregg Allman of the Allman Brothers Band, which hit all the gossip papers and magazines. She was also increasingly becoming known for wearing costumes on her show that were rather dramatic and outrageous, even outraging people by appearing on TV with her belly button exposed for all to see.

Yes, it did give Cher exposure (no pun intended), but it also opened her up to attacks by the rock establishment that considered such actions to be beneath them. Cher made a calculated swing towards disco in the later 1970's (although heavily rock-oriented) and signed with Casablanca in 1979, which appeared to some critics as a further sign that Cher wasn't with the "in crowd."

By 1980, however, Cher was willing to try something different — just as she had when she went from acting to singing, and from singing to television, and from ballads to disco. This time, she became the lead singer of a rock band called Black Rose, who released an album on Casablanca. It was a venture into hard rock. It made for a good album, but left fans adrift, unsure of what to make of Cher's new direction. She followed it up with a duet with Meatloaf for his DEAD RINGER album, which was another great rocker, but did little on the charts.

With so relatively little occurring for her on the music scene, Cher instead decided to give acting another try. After a successful theatrical run in Robert Altman's COME BACK TO THE FIVE AND DIME, JIMMY DEAN, JIMMY DEAN (and appearing in the film adaptation as well), Cher appeared in the film SILKWOOD. It was here that she ran into the same laughter and jokes that had haunted her other non-singing ventures. Still, nobody was laughing once they saw her performance in the film and she was nominated for an Oscar. This has led to her appearing in many films since then, and to her winning an acting Oscar for MOONSTRUCK.

Yet, it wasn't a case of giving up one role for another. Instead of sticking strictly with acting, Cher divided her time between movies and music. By 1989 she was back in the Top 10 with the single If I Could Turn Back Time. But the jokes still continued, now based on her dating a younger man and her video for the song which featured prominent exposure of Cher's tattoos and a lot of her body.

Yet, such taints have done little to dissuade Cher from continuing to explore new ground. She still refuses to slow down, continuing to act in films while still recording new singles and albums (including her 1998 No. 1 single Believe, making Cher the artist with the longest span between No. 1 hits and the oldest female artist to hit No. 1 on the rock charts).

But the jokes never went away and still continue today. Mainly as a bad habit of people who refuse to believe that Cher has represented and still represents someone who followed her own mind and didn't simply conform to the hipness that everyone else seemed to be following. Here was a woman who broke down the television wall by having her own successful variety series, something no other rock performer in the US could readily do (at least on US television). Cher also successfully dabbled in other genres of music over the years outside of what was thought "best" for her by the industry and public alike. She's certainly also been the most successful female rock singer in the movie industry over the years.

So let the jokes come. What the jokes do is provide something to say for those complainers who can't admit that Cher defied the taboos and broke down barriers that were unfairly restricting women rockers in the recording industry and beyond. And the jokes allow all the non-achievers to not have to admit that Cher has done a lot of popular work that still remains popular today. When the jokes have been forgotten, her accomplishments will still stand.

Best of the Studio Albums (as part of Sonny and Cher):
- LOOK AT US (Atco, 1965)
- BABY DON'T GO (Atco, 1965)
- GOOD TIMES (Atco, 1967)

Selected Studio Albums:
- ALL I REALLY WANT TO DO (Imperial, 1965)
- 3614 JACKSON HIGHWAY (Atco, 1969)
- GYPSYS, TRAMPS & THIEVES (MCA, 1971)
- HALF-BREED (MCA, 1973)
- DARK LADY (MCA, 1974)
- TAKE ME HOME (Casablanca, 1979)
- I PARALYZE (Columbia, 1982)
- CHER (Geffen, 1987)
- HEART OF STONE (Geffen, 1989)
- IT'S A MAN'S WORLD (WEA, 1996)
- BELIEVE (Warner Brothers, 1998)
- BLACK ROSE (EMI 1999, reissue of the album featuring Cher as vocalist from 1982)

Best of the "Best Of" Albums:
- GREATEST HITS (MCA, 1974)
- BANG BANG, MY BABY SHOT ME DOWN (EMI America, 1990)
- BEST OF CHER (EMI America, 1991)
- ORIGINAL HITS (Disky, 1998)
- IF I COULD TURN BACK TIME: GREATEST HITS (Geffen, 1999)

~ 11 ~
Petula Clark

Born November 15, 1932, Petula Clark became one of the most famous of the female vocalists to emerge from the early pop explosion of the 1960's. Clark, however, didn't quite follow in the foot steps of the many other women who came onto the rock scene in the late 1950's and early 60's, those such as Lesley Gore, Dusty Springfield or Brenda Lee. Unlike them, Clark was already a well-known singer in the UK years before she moved into the Rock and Roll genre.

Already recognized as a professional singer by the age of 10, Petula signed on with the British film studio, Rank Organization, in 1943 and spent many years appearing in films for them. This exposure led radio and to television, in addition to Petula already having recorded albums of dainty popular songs by the time she was 17. Her expansion into French recordings also helped her to gain popularity in other parts of Europe, but it was her switch to the emerging Rock and Roll style of music that cemented her place in history.

Doing variations of known hit material worked well for Petula, and she was very popular with the young generation that was soon to become fans of the Beatles — a remarkable accomplishment for an artist who was already in her 30's by the time of her biggest hit, *Downtown*, in 1964. *Downtown* was written and produced by Tony Hatch and not only became a huge hit for Clark in the UK, but was also the first (in 1965) No. 1 hit in the US for a British female singer in more than 12 years.

I Know a Place, her US follow-up to *Downtown*, hit No. 3 in the US and marked Petula Clark as the first female performer to hit the Top 3 with her first two singles in that country. In doing so, she established herself as the queen of the British Invasion, and was able to ride the tide of that association throughout the 1960's with continuous hits in both the US and the UK. She also continued her involvement with both television and movies, appearing in her own series in the UK, and doing a television special in the US (controversial at the time for a duet which featured her holding hands with Harry Belafonte). She also appeared in the film version of FINIAN'S RAINBOW and GOODBYE, MR. CHIPS.

As with many of the other female vocalists from the early 1960's, Clark's popularity diminished somewhat with the changes in the rock culture during the late 1960's. By 1975 her album recording career had slowed down considerably, although she was still very popular on television and on stage. The 1980's saw Petula return to the stage via the theater, first as Maria in a London production of THE SOUND OF MUSIC and then in a very well received production of BLOOD BROTHERS featuring Petula with David and Shawn Cassidy. Her work in the theater still continues. Petula appeared in the musical version of SUNSET BOULEVARD in the late 1990's.

To some, these diversions from the rock scene would suggest that Clark had had little impact on the overall look of rock music. But that would be very shortsighted. With her constant exposure on television, and as an already known star of films and television before her success with rock music, Petula Clark helped to push the envelope of rock music further by bringing a well-known face into the mix in the UK. Topping this off with her list of hits during the British Invasion years of the mid-1960's makes Petula's place secure in the history of rock music, and makes her a vital contributor in the defining the expanding role of female singers in the Rock and Roll world.

Selected Studio Albums:
- PET CLARK (Imperial, 1959)
- DOWNTOWN (Warner Brothers, 1964)
- UPTOWN WITH PETULA CLARK (Imperial, 1965)
- I COULDN'T LIVE WITHOUT YOUR LOVE (Warner Brothers, 1966)
- MY LOVE (Sequel, 1966)
- THESE ARE MY SONGS (Warner Brothers, 1967)
- JUST PETULA (Polygram, 1968)
- PETULA (Warner Brothers, 1968)
- OTHER MAN'S GRASS IS ALWAYS GREENER (Warner Brothers, 1968)
- JUST PET (Sequel, 1969)
- IN MEMPHIS (Warner Brothers, 1970)
- WARM AND TENDER (Sequel, 1971)
- TODAY (Sequel, 1971)
- NOW (MGM, 1972)
- COME ON HOME (Polygram, 1974)
- I'M THE WOMAN YOU NEED (Polygram, 1975)
- GIVE IT A TRY (Jango, 1986)
- DON'T SLEEP IN THE SUBWAY (RPM, 1995)

Best of the "Best Of" Albums:
- THE GREATEST HITS OF PETULA CLARK (GNP, 1986)
- THE CLASSIC COLLECTION (Pulse/Castle, 1999)
- DOWNTOWN: THE GREATEST HITS OF PETULA CLARK (Buddha, 1999)

Live Albums:
- LIVE AT THE ROYAL ALBERT HALL (GNP, 1972)
- LIVE IN LONDON (Polygram, 1974)
- LIVE AT THE COPACABANA (Sequel, 1986)

~ 12 ~
Ani Difranco

There's an up side and a down side to the corporate record game for an aspiring musician. On the one hand, you have the ability to be seen by millions of people at one time with the record label paying the bills. The label handles promotion, packaging and distribution — the business end — leaving the artist room to concentrate on putting on a show or recording another song. On the other hand, if someone else is footing the bill, they have a general right to make sure that the bill isn't going to be any bigger than it has too. Restrictions on what can be played or even said are just a small part of the overall picture (never mind the questions of how one may dress what songs will be recorded). However, for many who want to perform, the desire to be on a major label and gain the fame of success outweighs the possible restrictions placed on the art.

There were no arguments over art versus dollars when Ani DiFranco decided to record her first album. There were several contributing factors, but the most significant item may have been that she had already gained a level of success with her recordings before the labels had even heard of her.

Born September 23, 1970, Ani was pretty much left to her own devices growing up and by the age of nine had linked up with a group of singer / songwriters in the Buffalo, New York area. It was there that Ani felt the musical freedom of a musician being allowed to do what she want with her time and the freedom to create any type of music she desired. It was in this environment that Ani began composing songs at the age of 14. By the time she was 15, she was on her own, making a meager living performing acoustic guitar in folk clubs around the area.

At the age of 19 she had moved to New York, having built up a reputation in the club circuit for her innovative lyrics, strong vocals and guitar work. In response to fans' suggestion that she release some of her material on cassette or CD, Ani did just that — but not in the typical fashion of grooming herself for a label with demos. Instead, Ani cut out the middleman entirely and released the recordings herself on a cassette that she sold at shows in 1989. The tape sold so well that she decided to distribute her music on a more serious basis and founded her own company, Righteous Babe, for the distribution and handling of her albums.

Without the corporate motivations of "greatest profits at the least expense", Ani was able to record the music she wanted to without having to worry about changing tastes or the marketing ploys directed at new artists. She could also explore a wide variety of topics with her lyrics without worrying about upsetting the shirts at a large corporation. And in so doing, Ani was able to elevate her material to a more mature level than what other female artists in the alternate rock / folk genre were being permitted in the early 1990's. While most of her contemporaries were stuck singing about Teenage Angst and the Loneliness Of Love, Ani could move on to any topic she chose — discussions of relationships, abortion, gun-control, etc. Her musical style has also changed somewhat since the early albums: moving from a single acoustic guitar to a full band, and from a folk (albeit sometimes nearly hard rock) beat to a more Rock and Roll oriented structure.

With this freedom, Ani has been able to continually progress creatively and has gained a national and international audience for her music. Her albums have also made the move into the Top 100 album charts, which is very impressive for an independent label with one major artist.

So impressive in fact, that the labels finally took notice and tried to sign Ani up. Although the idea of being able to escape from the drudgery of paperwork probably had its appeal (along with some extra cash), Ani DiFranco was little interested in giving away the freedom that she had spent so long acquiring. Thus, she has and continues to turn down offers from outside labels and is still putting out her music herself. On the other side, many people tend to dwell only on the success of her business operation, giving little credence to the creativity of her music, thus missing the reason for starting the business in the first place — the music.

For some fans, it probably irks that other female artists get a lot of attention and fame while, at times, merely mirroring the hard work of Ani DiFranco. Certainly there are artists at top of the charts who would have a massive coronary if asked sing lyrics like DiFranco's, even though they're supposed to be so "antisocial" and "feminist." To have these others as household names while Ani's music remains on the fringe can certainly be a frustration (and the down side of doing things outside of the loop like Ani has). Yet, if it means that the fans will continue to get music from someone who's willing to sing what she feels instead of what's easy to sell, then true innovations in the music world will continue.

Selected Studio Albums:
- ◦ ANI DIFRANCO (Righteous Babe, 1989)
- ◦ NOT SO SOFT (Righteous Babe, 1991)
- ◦ IMPERFECTLY (Righteous Babe, 1992)
- ◦ PUDDLE DIVE (Righteous Babe, 1993)
- ◦ OUT OF RANGE (Righteous Babe, 1994)
- ◦ NOT A PRETTY GIRL (Righteous Babe, 1995)
- ◦ DILATE (Righteous Babe, 1996)
- ◦ MORE JOY, LESS SHAME (Righteous Babe, 1996)
- ◦ LITTLE PLASTIC CASTLE (Righteous Babe, 1998)
- ◦ UP UP UP UP UP UP (Righteous Babe, 1999)
- ◦ FELLOW WORKERS (Righteous Babe, 1999)
- ◦ TO THE TEETH (Righteous Babe, 1999)

Live Albums:
- ◦ LIVING IN CLIP (Righteous Babe, 1997)

~ 13 ~
Gloria Estefan

Gloria Estefan's career shows clearly that when an artist breaks through into other markets and reaches superstar status they're often labeled as a sellout by those who don't appreciate that doors have been opened. And when other artists will jump on the bandwagon and imitate the breakthrough artist, the imitators are often dumped on by those same audiences who were once their biggest fans. Fortunately, for Estefan, this attitude didn't last long when she "broke through" and did little damage to her career. The frustration of working as both an outsider and an insider in the eyes of the fans and the industry would make more than one performer want to throw up her hands and walk away.

Gloria Estefan was born Gloria Fajardo on September 1, 1957 in Havana, Cuba. Her family moved to Miami, Florida during Castro's takeover of Cuba two years later. Having to take care of the family while her mother worked, Gloria had picked up the guitar at the age of 14 and began to sing to pass the time. At the age of 17 she met Emilio Estefan, a musician who advised music students at Gloria's high school and was also performing dance music in a group called the Miami Latin Boys. The story gets a little fuzzy at this point in some sources, but Gloria had seen Emilio's band play at a wedding and was interested in singing with them. When Emilio decided that adding some women singers to the band would be a good commercial idea, he offered singing spots to both Gloria and her cousin Merci.

When Gloria learned of the job offer, she had second thoughts since she was going to the University of Miami for a degree in psychology and didn't want the fun she had singing to interfere with her studies. Her mother, however, convinced her to go ahead with the group as long as she kept it to weekends. With that, Gloria and Merci joined and the group's name was changed to The Miami Sound Machine.

Gloria earned her BA in psychology in 1978 — the same year that the band released its first album. The album, RENANCER, fit in perfectly with their live performances, being a combination of ballads and dance numbers in Spanish. It was a small start, but it was enough to eventually gain the attention of Discos CBS, a Miami-based division of CBS that specialized in music for the Hispanic population. After signing with them, The Miami Sound Machine recorded six albums with the label between 1979 and 1983 and hit the top of the charts in Latin America. Still, even with this success, the band was only known in pockets of the US because of the lack of promotion for their type of music in other parts of the country.

This changed in 1984 when CBS was convinced to release a single featuring a B-side called *Dr. Beat*. That song, sung in English, became a smash in Europe and convinced CBS to promote the next album aggressively for a possible crossover into the pop charts. The album, EYES OF INNOCENCE, did little better than the previous albums, but The Miami Sound Machine was increasing in popularity each time they appeared. So it was decided to once again get behind the band with the next album, 1986's PRIMITIVE LOVE.

PRIMITIVE LOVE became their true breakthrough in the US and also did well in Europe. Featuring *Conga* (the first song people who were not fans before probably heard) and *Bad Boy*, the album had not only an infectious beat, but the lyrics were joyous as well. Topped off with another hit single, Gloria's ballad *Words Get in the Way*, it was no wonder that the album eventually went Double Platinum.

With the album's breakthrough, Miami Sound Machine was able to successfully reintroduce dance music into the pop charts after a few years absense that followed the death of Disco in the very early 1980's (in fact, *Conga* was the first single to hit four US charts at the same time — Pop, Black, Dance and Latin). It also established Latin dance as the new sound to be embraced by pop artists, and several big names, including

Madonna, were soon using the Latin sound as if it were their own — varied and changed to their own tastes, but quite evidently based on the success of The Miami Sound Machine. This introduced many people in the US to the music coming out of the Hispanic community, and they developed a taste for music had typically been limited to dance radio stations. Although there were other performers who had gained success with the Latin style of music, Gloria and the MSM were one of the first to succeed in the rock and pop charts over an extended time period, proving that there was definitely a market for the Latin dance style in the pop world.

It's no wonder that Gloria became the center of attention when the group perfomed. After all, she was the lead singer, and so always in the limelight. She also was and is an attractive woman who knows how to communicate well with multi-lingual audiences in interviews, which she and Emilio did quite often in the following year.

In recognition of her emerging stardom, the band's name was changed to "Gloria Estefan And The Miami Sound Machine" in 1987. By 1989, the band's name no longer appeared on the front covers of albums (although they were certainly listed on the album jacket in the credits, etc.). Instead, the focus was completely on Gloria Estefan and her singing.

There was some backlash over this from fans who had followed the band in the early days and were seeing original members disappear as time went by. Even Emilio had gone on to the producer's role and was no longer among the musicians playing on the albums. This feeling of leaving things behind also contributed to accusations that Gloria was pandering to the US Pop market and not directly addressing the Latin market any longer. Built on the notion that the albums were becoming increasingly pop (and ballad) oriented and heavily in English, there were some who criticized Gloria for forsaking the very fans on whom their success had been built.

While there may have been some justification in the issue of former band members fading in the light of Gloria's star status, the "not Latin" criticisms can't be supported. Not only had Gloria continued to do Latin flavored music on her albums (or revised material to give it more of a Latin beat), she had also contributed entire albums to Latin music, including MI TIERRA in 1993 and ABRIENDO PUERTAS. Meanwhile, the wannabe pop artists who were using some of the same sounds in their music never faced the heat as Gloria did.

But Gloria took the criticisms as well as could be expected and they did little to affect her popularity. Although faced with a few personal crises over the years (including a nearly crippling accident that led to spinal surgery in 1991), Gloria continues to do exceedingly well in her craft and in her popularity. Thanks to that success, she opened the doors for other Latin artists to prove that playing this type of rock-related music doesn't have to be a one hit wonder accomplishment.

Selected Studio Albums:
- RIO (Disco CBS, 1978)
- EYES OF INNOCENCE (Epic, 1984)
- PRIMITIVE LOVE (Epic, 1986)

- A TODA MAQUINA (Epic, 1986)
- ANYTHING FOR YOU (Epic, 1988)
- LET IT LOOSE (Epic, 1988)
- CUTS BOTH WAY (Epic, 1989)
- INTO THE LIGHT (Epic, 1991)
- MI TIERRA (Epic, 1993)
- HOLD ME THRILL ME KISS ME (Epic, 1994)
- CHRISTMAS THROUGH YOUR EYES (Epic, 1995)
- ABRIENDO PUERTAS (Epic, 1995)
- DESTINY (Epic, 1996)
- GLORIA! (Epic, 1998)

Best of the "Best Of" Albums:
- GREATEST HITS (Epic, 1992)
- 20TH ANNIVERSARY (Sony, 1999)

~ 14 ~
Melissa Etheridge

The late 1980's were a more difficult time than usual to land a record contract in the rock music world. The popular styles of the late 1980's seem to stress performers who were either into heavy metal or some type of dance music. There were a few artists in-between, but they were mostly a middle-of-the-road collection of pop artists with mellow sounds who managed to segregate themselves by not being near either of the extremes. Into this mix came Melissa Etheridge, who wanted a career as a Rock and Roll singer / guitarist.

Melissa was born on May 29, 1961 in Leavenworth, Kansas and was given a guitar at the age of eight by her parents. From then on music was her life, and after attending Berklee College of Music for a time in Boston, Melissa decided it was time to break into the music business. It was 1982 and new wave was at the crest of the music in the Boston area, which held little interest for Melissa. Figuring Los Angeles would be geared more towards the Rock and Roll sound of performers like Bonnie Raitt and Bruce Springsteen that she enjoyed playing, she arrived in LA on her 21st birthday only to find that the growing heavy metal scene was developing there instead. Instead of the rock sound she expected to find, many of the top clubs were playing heavy metal exclusively. Wanting to play her own music live, she searched for smaller clubs in the Los Angeles area willing to let her perform, leading to a slow but steady fanbase by the mid-1980's.

She was eventually signed to Island Records, and her first album was released in 1988. The album featured her first hit, *Give Me Some Water*, and break into the Top 25 albums chart, propelling Etheridge into the national limelight. Again, at a time when the music being played on the radio stations and MTV was almost exclusively metal and rap,

Etheridge's music was a more rock-oriented sound evincing clear lyrical directions. In essence, it was good old fashion rock music. Even though MTV and most radio stations took little notice (her videos typically ran on the "older audience" oriented VH1 video network), the audience for Melissa's music was growing, in response, perhaps, to the overall lack of good rock music at that time. People were also attracted to Melissa's vocals which had a gutsy, hardened tone very reminiscent of Janis Joplin (whom Etheridge had mention time and again as one of her favorites).

Courtesy Rock Classics

Etheridge followed up the first album with BRAVE AND CRAZY in 1989, reached the Top 25 and remained on the charts for over a year. This was followed in 1992 with NEVER ENOUGH and 1993's YES I AM, both of which continued her classic rock stylings. In the early 1990's the metal phase had died and grunge and alternative rock took over. Many new singer / songwriter artists appeared at that time (and many with a guitar strapped on) who almost universally got stuck with the alternative rock label, but Melissa wasn't tossed into that crowd. Instead, she remained somewhat an outsider — playing rock music with straightforward narrative lyrics and continuing to do well on the charts.

In 1999, Melissa released another new album, BREAKDOWN, which once again earned a prominent position on the charts. Her continued success delivers a clear message to other performers — you don't have to jump on the bandwagon to find success in the music world. And there's another message there too — that straight ahead Rock and Roll music is still something that people will go out of their way to listen to and enjoy.

Selected Studio Albums:
- MELISSA ETHERIDGE (Island, 1988)
- BRAVE AND CRAZY (Island, 1989)
- NEVER ENOUGH (Island, 1992)
- YES I AM (Island, 1993)
- YOUR LITTLE SECRET (Island, 1995)
- BREAKDOWN (Polygram, 1999)

~ 15 ~
Marianne Faithfull

Marianne Faithfull is a perfect example of how sometimes an artist does her best work after most people have already written her off. Although starting as a singer in the Dusty Springfield / Petula Clark mode in the mid-1960's, by the end of the 1970's she had been accepted as a forerunner of the introspective songwriters who would flood the rock genre by the end of the 1980's. She could even be considered an early voice in the post-punk / riot grrrl genre.

Born December 29, 1946, Marianne had aspirations to become a singer, and through her boyfriend, John Dunbar, she met Andrew Loog Oldham, the manager of the Rolling Stones. Oldham took seriously her wanting to become a singer and got Marianne a deal with Decca Records. Mick Jagger and Keith Richards wrote her first single, *As Tears Go By* which was also her first hit. From there she was another darling of the rock music set in the UK and released a variety of singles over the next few years. She was also becoming known as a notorious party girl, especially after the 1967 drug raid at Keith Richard's house that supposedly found her naked in a bathtub.

She had become Jagger's girlfriend by the late 1960's and had reached the point of having a "best of" album release in 1969, but that was also the year that things starting going sour. After surviving a coma, induced by an overdose, she sought help for a heroin addiction. She also found her creative energy gone, not recording another album until 1977 (although she did appear in David Bowie's 1973 MIDNIGHT SPECIAL television special in a nun's habit to sing *I've Got You Babe* with Bowie's Ziggy Stardust).

The albums released in 1977 and 1978, DREAMING MY DREAMS and FAITHLESS, did only so-so on the charts, but they were signs of what was to come. Writing her own material more and more, Faithfull began to find out how much she had to say, and what she had to say was taking on a more aggressive and punk-like edge than anything that she had been involved with in the 1960's (with the possible exception of *Sister Morphine* in 1969). In essence, these two albums were just Faithfull's training wheels for what was to become the album that she will undoubtedly be remembered most for, BROKEN ENGLISH, in 1979.

The album propelled Marianne Faithfull back into the limelight and showed a singer who had lost the innocent voice of her youth to a world-weary and deeper voice. It fit in well with her new material, which dug deeper into her own personal wounds as well as addressing the world at large. The album did well and formed a new image of Faithfull as the Marlene Dietrich of the Rock and Roll world.

BROKEN ENGLISH was followed by several other in the 1980's and 90's, each exploring more areas of her writing abilities, but none quite matching the explosiveness of her 1979 work. Surprisingly, when people had figured that she was just a party girl who had had one too many, she showed them that there was always a chance to come back — and that each lesson learned is yet another story waiting to be told.

Selected Studio Albums:
- ○ MARIANNE FAITHFULL (London, 1965)
- ○ COME MY WAY (Decca, 1965)
- ○ GO AWAY FROM MY WORLD (London, 1965)
- ○ NORTH COUNTRY MAID (Decca, 1966)
- ○ FAITHFUL FOREVER (London, 1966)
- ○ LOVE IN A MIST (Decca, 1967)
- ○ THE WORLD OF MARIANNE FAITHFULL (Decca, 1969)
- ○ DREAMING MY DREAMS (NEMS, 1977)
- ○ FAITHLESS (Sony, 1978)
- ○ BROKEN ENGLISH (Island, 1979)
- ○ DANGEROUS ACQUAINTANCES (Island, 1981)
- ○ A CHILD ADVENTURE (Island, 1983)
- ○ STRANGE WEATHER (Island, 1987)
- ○ A SECRET LIFE (Island, 1995)
- ○ 20TH CENTURY BLUES (RCA, 1997)
- ○ THE SEVEN DEADLY SINS (RCA, 1998)
- ○ VAGABOND WAYS (IT, 1999)

Best of the "Best Of" Albums:
- ○ MARIANNE FAITHFULL'S GREATEST HITS (ABKCO, 1987)
- ○ A COLLECITON OF HER BEST RECORDINGS (Island, 1995)
- ○ PREFECT STRANGE: THE ISLAND ANTHOLOGY (Polygram, 1998)

Live Albums:
- ○ BLAZING AWAY (Island, 1997)

~ 16 ~
Lita Ford

A few months ago when my latest book came out, a box of the newly released book arrived at home and I had grabbed a couple of copies and went over a friend's place to show it to her. She looked it over and then asked, "So, what's your next book?"

I immediately told her I was working on a different kind of music book this time, one dealing with the most influential women rockers of the 20th Century. I then explained that I planned on covering a large assortment of performers from the early days of rock to heavy metal, punk, etc. I had spent the previous few days working on a list of performers that would fit the bill as being chiefly influential to rock music. I had worked on it for so long that, if asked, the names would practically roll off my tongue. There was Janis and Madonna and Tori and Stevie and Dusty and —

"So, is Lita Ford going to be in there?"

I sputtered. "Uh, well, I had thought about covering Joan Jett, but I thought I would cover most of the heavy metal aspects with Wendy O. Williams, and . . ."

"Oh, you've got to cover Lita. Everybody remembers her. I mean she was one of the main stars of heavy metal back in the 1980's."

"Uh," I hesitated. "Um . . . I'll think about it."

* * *

Rosanna Ford was born September 19, 1958 (some sources say 1959) in London, England. However, her British heritage had little time to take root since her family emigrated to the US when she was still a child. Instead, she ended up in California where she began to play the guitar at the age of 11. By 16 she was good enough that she was already beginning to think about making music her career.

As it happened, 1975 was a good year to think about doing so. With the success of Suzi Quatro over in Europe and the imposing image of a young women playing hard Rock and Roll music, famous musician and producer Kim Fowley got a bright idea — if one girl on stage created this much of a reaction, just think how successful a whole band of girls would be. Finding a group of underage girls to perform the music would be a real accomplishment. And, of course, after actually having found them, calling them The Runaways only added (from a marketing standpoint) what would just had to be a winner.

While Fowley may not have had the purest of intentions musically with his plan (seeing them more as a product than a band), his ability to find talent was definite. Working throughout 1975, he managed to pull together a band that included a lot of talent in addition to Ford, who was now going by the name of Lita. There was Joan Jett, two years younger than Ford but with the same desire to succeed. Now add in the singing abilities of Cherrie Curie, who had a tremendous stage presence. A bassist and drummer soon followed to round out the group, Jackie Fox and Sandy West, who were no slouches either. The five truly and successfully gelled together into a band. The focus was on hard rock, with a touch of punk in the mix as well. What they were was a band that played simple, solid Rock and Roll, and their first three albums (THE RUNAWAYS, QUEEN OF NOISE and WAITIN' FOR THE NIGHT) are essential albums for fans of the early punk / heavy metal movement of the late 1970's, especially those looking for the movement's women rockers.

Fowley was correct about one thing: the band was a success. Unfortunately, The Runaways' success, like the earlier success of Suzi Quatro, came in Europe and Japan, but not in the US. Still, the band released their first album in 1976 and begin touring overseas. By 1977, however, they were already starting to shift wildly and out of control. In July 1977 Jackie Fox left the band, and in August she was followed by the band's central figure, Cherrie Currie (who would record two excellent albums on her own, BEAUTY'S ONLY SKIN DEEP and MESSIN' WITH THE BOYS). The Runaways continued with Joan Jett taking over vocals and replacement performers being found, but by the end of 1978 the band was really on its last legs.

By the beginning of 1979, both Lita and Joan saw the band possibly continuing, but the differing directions that they wanted to go in was the split that ended the band. While Joan felt that a more permanent move towards a Ramones Rock and Roll sound for the band was what was needed, Lita felt heavy metal was the way to go. Neither could be converted to the other's point of view and Lita left the band soon after. Joan, of course, went her own way, but more about her later in the book.

* * *

A few months into the writing of this book, I went to visit my folks for a weekend. At dinner, my mom asked me what the next book was about.

"Women in rock, Mom," I said, trying to talk through the strings of spaghetti in my mouth.

"Oh, who's in it," Mom enquired.

Thinking of women rockers that she might have known I quickly mentioned Tina Turner, Brenda Lee and Cher.

"Oh," my Mom said. "Will you be talking about Lita Ford?"

courtesy Hot Wacks

I choked down my food. "Lita Ford? Mom, how do you know about Lita Ford?"

My Mom looked at me with a shrug. "Just a name I remembered, that's all. I remember she used to have videos on that MTV channel you used to watch."

"Man," I muttered, returning to my dinner. "Lita Ford. I'll think about adding her."

* * *

Although The Runaways had given Lita a taste of success, it didn't put food on the table, and she found herself working at a variety of jobs over the next five years while perfecting her music and her vocal abilities. By 1983, she was able to swing a deal with Mercury Records and recorded her first solo album, OUT FOR BLOOD. It was a minor success in the charts, but it was a significant early success for a female heavy metal artist (who were definintely few and far between at that time). While Wendy O. Williams was starting to gear her music more towards the growing heavy metal movement (revived by the punk scene and the success of British hard rock bands like Iron Maiden and Judas Priest), she was still comfortably in the punk realm. Lee Aaron was known in some circles, but more as a pin-up girl for the movement than for her music. Girlschool was one of the very few female acts that had managed to make a dent, but that was a band, not a solo performer. OUT FOR BLOOD was a hard rock album by a solo woman performer — and the video for the title track sparked controversy by being considered too violent for most music channels.

With her new notoriety, Lita came back the following year with the album that was to be the breakthrough album of her career, DANCING ON THE EDGE. She was now considered a major heavy metal talent in a genre that was becoming one of the major rock movements of the 1980's. She began touring in the US (along with Europe) and was recording her third album for Mercury, THE BRIDE WORE BLACK, when she decided to move from Mercury to RCA. It would be four years before her next album came out.

* * *

Working on a charity music project for a group out in California, I became friendly with the woman producing the project. Her job also included performing, recording and producing a music CD that was included with the project, so I thought she would be interested in knowing about the "Women in Rock" book.

"You're including Lita, of course, right?" Those were the first words she said after hearing about the project.

"That's it! What is it about Lita Ford that makes her the first person people think of when I mention this project. You're the tenth person who immediately thought of Lita Ford when they heard about this book. Why is that?"

My producer friend responded, "Well, she really was an inspiration to a lot of girls who were growing up at the time that wanted to play music. Who wanted to play hard rock."

"But there were other women out there."

"Yeah, but they were in bands with a lot of other band members. Here was Lita out on her own. She was the focus and she played music that women weren't supposed to be playing. The spotlight was on her. She was one of the true women success stories for heavy metal. That's why women look up to her. That's why you've got to cover her."

My stubbornness at refusing to cover Lita because people kept dropping her name was erased.

"Okay, you're right. After all, if it's a name everyone thinks of when I mention the book there's got to be something there."

* * *

1988 saw the release of LITA, the album that broke Lita Ford into the Top 40 in the US with the help of her first single off the album, *Kiss Me Deadly*. The single reached No. 12 and the album No. 29. She followed that success with a duet with Ozzy Osbourne on the song *Close My Eyes Forever*, which reached No. 8 in mid-1989.

courtesy KAOS2000

At that point Lita had reached what became the height of her career. While the follow-up albums, SITLETTO (1990) and DANGEROUS CURVES (1991) were successful with fans, they showed a steady decline on the charts. This was mostly a reflection of the shift by fans who wanted to move with the times and abandoned heavy metal for the grunge and alternative movements that had begun their stranglehold on American youth. By the time her 1995 album, BLACK, was released on the small ZYX label, there was little room for heavy metal on the charts — at least not like that of the 1980's.

For the moment, Lita continues to work on new music and stays with the brand of hard rock that she perfected in the 1980's. 2000 has seen some continued talks of a new album, and there still remains interest in Lita becuase of her past success. So much so that BMC reissued her GREATEST HITS album in 1999. In the meantime, Lita is still looked upon as a winner in a music genre that left scant room for women to succeed.

* * *

I was called into a one-on-one meeting with my boss a couple of months back. My boss, a women about the same age as I, was finishing up some suggestions for the new year and I was getting ready to leave her office when the talk turned to my writing projects.

"So, I hear you're working on a book about women in music," she said as she went over her notes.

"Yes," I said. "It's about women in rock music."

She looked up from her papers with a look of concern on her face.

"PLEASE tell me you won't be covering Lita Ford."

"Uh . . ."

"I couldn't stand her. I couldn't stand her music. Please tell me you won't cover her in the book."

"Uh, um . . . I'll think about it."

With that I made a hasty exit from the office.

Selected Studio Albums (as part of the Runaways):
- RUNAWAYS (Touchwood 1976)
- QUEENS OF NOISE (Touchwood 1977)
- WAITIN' FOR THE NIGHT (Mercury 1977)
- AND NOW THE RUNAWAYS (Cherry Red 1980)
- FLAMIN' SCHOOLGIRLS (Cherry Red 1980)
- LITTLE LOST GIRLS (Cherry Red 1981)
  (It should be noted that only the first three albums were released during Lita Ford's time in the band. All other albums were released using material recorded from early recording sessions.)

Selected Studio Albums:
- OUT FOR BLOOD (Mercury, 1983)
- DANCIN' ON THE EDGE (Mercury, 1984)
- LITA (Dreamland, 1988)
- STILETTO (RCA, 1990)
- DANGEROUS CURVES (RCA, 1991)
- BLACK (ZYX, 1995)

Live Album (as part of the Runaways):
- LIVE IN JAPAN (Mercury, 1977)

Best of the "Best Of" Albums:
- THE BEST OF LITA FORD (Dreamland, 1992)
- GREATEST HITS (BMG, 1999)
- THE BEST OF THE RUNAWAYS (Mercury, 1987)

~ 17 ~
Aretha Franklin

Performers that have been around for more than five years or so usually have a discography that shows periods of relative inactivity. As with some of the performers included in this book, there could be long periods with no new recordings while an opportunity outside of an artist's usual genre is being explored, or even something outside music altogether. One glance at Aretha Franklin's career would cause you to assume that she rarely had time to even sit down, much less do anything outside of her music career.

Born March 25, 1942 in Memphis, Tennessee, Aretha spent most of her early years in Detroit, Michigan where her father had moved the family. Her father, the Reverend C. L. Franklin, was pastor of the New Bethel Church and was quite well-known by the early 1950's as a man who knew how to deliver a sermon — he was even recorded by Chess Records and commanded thousands of dollars per sermon.

It was in the church that Aretha became interested in music. With the church doing well and gospel music filling the air, provided by such singers are Marion Williams, Mahalia Jackson and Clara Ward, Aretha felt that singing was her goal in life. So much so that still at an early age she was already singing in the church and by the age of 14 she had recorded her first album of gospel music for the Checker label.

So, Aretha knew that music and singing were going to be her life, but she never thought much of performing music outside of gospel until she saw Sam Cooke. Seeing and hearing Cooke perform at the church one night and then do a secular set at a club the next day, Franklin realized that she could sing anything she wanted to and didn't have to be pinned down to a particular format of music if she didn't wish to be.

From Detroit, Franklin went to New York and recorded demos, which were picked up by Columbia Records. Signing a contract with the label, Aretha and Columbia believed at the time that it was the start of great things for everyone involved.

Which was not quite the case. Sticking with a mixture of gospel, slow pop standards and jazz, Aretha spent five years at Columbia and had several albums under her belt when she and the label came to a mutual agreement to part ways. Feeling that the parade was passing her by, Franklin instead went to Atlantic Records and found producers there that were interested in allowing her some freedom in picking out material for her albums.

It was at Atlantic that Aretha's career really took off. With the R&B song *I Never Loved a Man (the Way I Love You)*, Aretha had a song that was heating up the radio stations long before a second track could be recorded for use as a single. The song reached No. 9 on the pop charts and was followed that same year (1967) with a cover of Otis Redding's *Respect*, which did even better, reaching No. 1 and making her place as a new singer to look out for on the charts.

With a strong voice that reached out and grabbed the listener, and earned her the nickname Lady Soul, Aretha captivated rock music fans and soul fans alike — during a period where the term "rock music" was encompassing a varied collection of musical genres: rock, pop, soul and even some of the country flavored tunes. When *Respect* was followed by the No. 4 single *Baby I Love You*, it seemed that Aretha couldn't lose. There was certainly no denying it once after seeing that there was rarely a single from Franklin that didn't hit the charts, and that many of them reached the Top 10.

The late 1960's and early 70's witnessed Franklin recording hit after hit for Atlantic, and rarely being away from the studio and the charts (she did take a brief break from the end of 1969 through the middle of 1970). She also continued winning regular awards as the years went by. And yet, just as the number of awards was reaching epic proportions, a shift occurred in the world of rock music and things began to fragment. Listeners were once again each typically adhering to a single musical genre, unlike the mixed listening they were doing earlier in the 1970's. With this change, recording artists were trapped into trying to anticipate the next popular style in order to stay current, and were all too often entirely unsure of in which direction to go. And, of course, those who's styles or abilities didn't allow them to adapt quickly quickly became histroy.

Aretha had to face this struggle. She tried moving to disco styled material in the latter 1970's, but as time passed her record sales, both singles and albums, were slowing. So, in 1980 she decided she needed to break away and find fresh fields for her career. Moving from Atlantic to Arista Records, Aretha made a comeback with the album JUMP TO IT in 1982, which reached No. 23 on the charts. It was followed in 1985 with the album WHO'S ZOOMIN' WHO?, which hit No. 13 (and included hit singles that reached even higher).

From there, Aretha worked in a variety of musical fields, and her albums can attest to the fact that she's never happier than when she's trying new material or a new genre different from what she's done before. To some eyes that can be read as a sign of desperation, but what it actually shows is a singer who simply wants to sing a variety of music and not be trapped into a single genre as happens to so many. So Aretha's career has expanded through many genres and she's one of the very few women singers who've managed to take hold in all of the soul, R&B and rock genres. She's respected in all of those fields because, unlike those who've had one or two crossover hits, she's had hit songs that have concurrently climbed the charts of multiple genres, and has done so over and over again.

Because of all this, Aretha Franklin is considered to be an icon of the pop world. And nothing seems to be slowing down — she continues to go wherever she aims, and will probably to do for many years to come.

Selected Studio Albums:
- THE GOSPEL SOUL OF ARETHA FRANKLIN (Checker, 1956)
- THE ELECTRIFYING ARETHA FRANKLIN (Columbia, 1962)
- SONGS OF FAITH (Checker, 1964)
- ARETHA ARRIVES (Atlantic, 1967)
- I NEVER LOVED A MAN (THE WAY I LOVE YOU) (Atlantic, 1967)
- ARETHA NOW (Atlantic, 1968)
- QUEEN OF SOUL (Harmony, 1968)
- LADY SOUL (Atlantic, 1968)
- SOUL '69 (Atlantic, 1969)
- SPIRIT IN THE DARK (Atlantic, 1970)
- YOUNG, GIFTED & BLACK (Atlantic, 1971)
- HEY NOW HEY (Atlantic, 1973)
- WITH EVERYTHING I FEEL IN ME (Atlantic, 1974)
- YOU (Atlantic, 1975)
- SWEET PASSION (Atlantic, 1977)
- LA DIVA (Atlantic, 1979)
- ARETHA SINGS THE BLUES (Columbia, 1980)
- JUMP TO IT (Arista, 1982)
- WHO'S ZOOMIN' WHO? (Arista, 1985)
- ARETHA (Arista, 1986)
- WHAT YOU SEE IS WHAT YOU SWEAT (Arista, 1991)
- JAZZ TO SOUL (Columbia, 1992)
- UNFORGETTABLE: A TRIBUTE TO DINAH WASHINGTON (Columbia, 1995)
- A ROSE IS STILL A ROSE (Arista, 1998)

Best of the "Best Of" Albums:
- THE BEST OF ARETHA FRANKLIN (Atlantic, 1968)
- ARETHA'S GOLD (Atlantic, 1969)
- THE LEGENDARY QUEEN OF SOUL (CBS, 1983)
- 30 GREATEST HITS (Atlantic, 1986)
- QUEEN OF SOUL: THE ATLANTIC RECORDINGS (Rhino, 1993)

Live Albums:
- ARETHA IN PARIS (Atlantic, 1968)
- ARETHA FRANKLIN: LIVE! (Hallmark, 1969)
- ARETHA LIVE AT FILLMORE WEST (Atlantic, 1971)

~ 18 ~
Lesley Gore

Another star of the early 1960's, Lesley Gore was one of the best known in a period when women singers were just beginning to establish careers based on a rocking pop sound. As with many of the others, she also foud herself on the way out by the end of the 1960's. But there's more to Lesley Gore's story than being a mere blip in Rock and Roll history.

Born May 2, 1946 in New York, Gore's pre-stardom musical history wasn't very different from the average aspiring singer or performer. By the age of 16, Lesley was singing with a jazz group in Manhattan and her vocal coach decided to send a demo tape of the band to Irving Green, the president of Mercury Records. Although Green saw little possibility for the band itself, he was impressed enough with Gore's singing abilities to sign her to a Mercury contract.

Percieving a need for someone to coach Gore through her early recording experience, Green picked an up-and-coming staff producer by the name of Quincy Jones to work with her. Jones, seeing how the girl group movement (almost single-handedly produced by Phil Spector) was a phenomenon on to itself, decided that Gore's first single would be a great way to explore these same waters. Using a multi-track method of recording, Jones managed to turn Gore into a girl group all by herself and her first single, *It's My Party*, leapt up the charts to No. 1 by June 1963 (and reached a respectable No. 9 on the UK charts).

Gore and Jones worked together on similar material embracing the girl group genre, and Gore's place in pop rock history would have been ensured by this alone, but 1964 she released another smash hit, and one that had a life outside of the girl group genre, *You Don't Own Me*. At the time, the song was considered somewhat feminist, but more importantly it contained Gore's vibrant soaring vocal, which was a definite break away from the typical "I want my boyfriend" type of material at the core of the typical girl group song.

She continued to have hits throughout most of the early- to mid-1960's (with and without Jones, who had moved on to other performers after working with Gore), but like many of the female vocalists who surfaced in the early 60's, she experienced waning interest as musical styles and tastes began changing. Gore, however, had an ace up her sleeve. She was able to keep her career moving throughout the remainder of the 60's with her ability to write songs as well as she could perform them. Whereas other singers became known for their ability to interpret material in their own fashion, Gore had taken an active part in the writing of the songs for her albums in the mid-to late- 1960's and continued writing songs from that point forward.

Which is the other legacy of Lesley Gore — a girl group-style singer who embraced the creative side of her music as well as performing it. Being as young and stereotyped as Lesley was, people forget that she wrote a lot of her material herself. Doing so at a time when a singer was thought of as merely a singer — another instrument to be played — instead of an active part of the

creative process, writing her own material was a big step down the path to the performers of today who typically write and play their own music, rarely covering another's material.

No doubt, Lesley Gore will always be remembered as the *It's My Party* girl, but those who dig a little deeper will find her history impressive and realize that she helped to shape the world of Rock and Roll music.

Selected Studio Albums:
- I'LL CRY IF I WANT TO (Mercury, 1963)
- SONGS OF MIXED UP HEARTS (Mercury, 1963)
- BOYS, BOYS, BOYS (Mercury, 1964)
- GIRL TALK (Mercury, 1964)
- MY TOWN, MY GUY & ME (Mercury, 1965)
- SINGS ALL ABOUT LOVE (Mercury, 1966)
- CALIFORNIA NIGHTS (Mercury, 1967)
- LOVE, LOVE, LOVE (Wing, 1968)
- SOUND OF YOUNG LOVE (Wing, 1969)
- SOMEPLACE ELSE NOW (MoWest, 1972)
- LOVE ME BY NAME (A&M, 1975)

Best of the "Best Of" Albums:
- THE GOLDEN HITS OF LESLEY GORE, VOL. 1 & 2 (Mercury, 1965/68)
- ANTHOLOGY (Rhino, 1986)
- SUNSHINE, LOLLIPOPS & RAINBOWS: THE BEST OF LESLEY GORE (Rhino, 1998)

~ 19 ~
Nina Hagen

Sometimes the US pop culture does an injustice in not recognizing the role of foreign artists when discussing changes in musical genres. Typically, when excavating the history of a musical form, writers tend to look for direct links right here in the US, little taking note of influences from outside of the country, or only going as far as the UK, our direct link to Europe. In doing so, they tend to take for granted other artists (living in other parts of the world) who perhaps had a greater influence on a genre.

Nina Hagen certainly fits into the class of overlooked-in-the-US. Creating a dark web of music in the mid-1970's, she was often at that time listed as an early punk queen. With a more electronic-oriented sound, combined with a pounding rhythm, her music influenced many of the female artists of the punk, post-punk and alternative periods (whether they realize it or not). After a relatively brief sojourn through the mass-media world, Nina returned to Germany and has since been little seen outside the German market (although she still records today).

courtesy Hot Wacks

Born in Berlin, Germany on March 11, 1955, Nina first appeared in public after being exiled from East Germany and emigrating to the West in 1976. It was there that she formed a band to attempt material that could only be described as electronic punk. They were signed to CBS Germany and their first album was released in 1978, titled NINA HAGEN BAND. They were little heard outside of Germany, but the record did well enough to warrant a second album in 1980, UNBEHAGEN.

By that time, Nina's flamboyant style, both in concert and on record, had gained them a cult following in those corners of the planet wanting to experience European punk music. It was enough for CBS to give a sampling of the material a shot in the US, and an EP of four songs from the first two albums was released in 1980. When that showed signs of selling, Nina arrived in

New York to record her first English language album, NUNSEXMONKROCK in 1982. It was followed in 1983 by the album FEARLES, which charted with the Top 10 dance hit *New York New York*

She recorded one more album for CBS in 1985, IN EKSTASE, but her popularity in the US was never anything like what she had enjoyed in Germany, so she returned home in the mid-1980's. Since then, she has continued to record albums for the German market and has also moved on to film appearances. Her career seems assured in the country of her birth, but we can always hope that the rest of the world may get to hear another Nina Hagen hit some day.

Selected Studio Albums:
- NINA HAGEN BAND (Baktabak, 1979)
- UNBEHAGEN (CBS, 1980)
- NINA HAGEN BAND EP (CBS, 1980)
- NUNSEXMONKROCK (CBS, 1982)
- ANGSTLOS (CBS, 1983)
- FEARLESS (CBS, 1983)
- IN EKSTASE (Baktabak, 1985)
- NINA HAGEN (Mercury, 1989)
- STREET (Polydor, 1991)
- REVOLUTION BALLROOM (European Import, 1993)
- FRE (D) EUCH (RCA, 1995)
- OM NAMAH SHIVAY (Biem/Gema, 1999)
- RETURN OF THE MOTHER (BMG, 2000)

Best of the "Best Of" Albums:
- BEST OF NINA HAGEN (Alex, 1991)
- DEFINITIVE COLLECTION (Alex, 1995)

~ 20 ~
Debbie Harry

Most of the performers listed in this book are artists known primarily for their solo work, and while Debbie Harry is best recognized as one part of Blondie, there's much in her career that was influential — influential not only to other women rockers, but also to the gradual transition from the punk era to new wave, and from new wave to the electronic pop rock of the mid-1980's. Of course, some tend to dismiss Harry's work as having being around for a only short time, but her vocals were of a unique style that still hasn't been imitated successfully. Meanwhile, the innovations that Blondie purveyed are almost like a blueprint for the rock scene from the mid-1970's through the mid-80's.

And further, Debbie has continued to work on solo projects, both music and other creative endeavors, which have enlarged the public's previously limited concepts of what a women rock singer could do. Her's has certainly been a career that departed from the common path of so many other women from the punk / new wave era. Whether Debbie was happy about it or not, she became the icon of the new wave movement very early on, and it's stuck with her to the present day. Debbie had unintentionally acquired the image of a new wave Marilyn Monroe (years before Madonna began cultivating that image in the public eye), and, as with most icons, she'd never planned it that way.

courtesy Hot Wacks

Born July 1, 1945 in Miami, Florida, Debbie was adopted at the age of three by a couple in Hawthorne, New Jersey. Growing up in the Northeast, she went through school in a typical fashion, and by the late 1960's she was working as the singer in a short-lived folk rock band called Wind In The Willows. After the band went nowhere, Debbie spent her time in the New York City area working in clubs such as CBGB, and for a short while as a Bunny in one of the Playboy Clubs. All the while she kept working in music and finally put together a girl group trio called The Stilettos, and played in CBGB and other clubs in the early 1970's.

Melissa Etheridge

Chrissie Hynde

Sarah Mclachlan

As it happens, New York was the first true fertile ground for the movement that became punk, and The Stilettos were as much involved with the new music as any of the other groups out of the New York scene. However, by 1974 The Stilettos were pretty much on their way out and Harry had met up with a guitarist by the name of Chris Stein. Still using some of the old girl group material from The Stilettos' sets, the band began as Angel And The Snake, but they later changed their name to Blondie.

The band went through several changes during its early years, but the core of the group always remained Harry and Stein. They gradually developed a following and then landed a record deal.

courtesy Hot Wacks

In 1976 their first album, BLONDIE, was released on a small label called Private Stock. The album did as well as anyone would expect from a small label, but it attracted attention in the UK, where it was considered a bit more artistically innovative than some of the punk albums hitting the market at the time. For this reason, Chrysalis showed interest in the band and eventually pick up their contract from Private Stock for the release of their second album, PLASTIC LETTERS.

PLASTIC LETTERS hit the Top 10 in the UK and make it to No. 72 on the US charts. As the punk movement began to sweep the US in the late 1970's, more and more attention was being given to to Harry and Blondie as an example of what to expect. However, this sort of thinking was typical of the rash judgements aimed at punk in those days. While the band's early material was more punk-oriented, by the time of their third release in 1978, PARALLEL LINES, they had evolved into the more electronic rock style that came to be identified as the new wave movement. It was with the third album that their popularity really grew, thanks in part to the innovations of ever more promotional films for their singles. With Debbie's startlingly looks, her unique singing style, and the innovative music, which was still largely unheard in many corners of the US, listeners and viewers alike were swept away by the band. With all of this in addition to the attention that Debbie Harry was getting in the Andy Warhol's domains in the New York area, it was little wonder that Blondie became very popular.

Or that Debbie herself became so popular. While the band really did work as a band — with writing and performing shared by all — the focus of the band was on the lead singer, who also their spokesperson. With Blondie's rise in popularity on the crest of the new wave movement, Harry's place as the queen of that movement was pretty much assured. The band's attempts to focus the public's attention on the BAND instead of the SINGER, were generally either ignored or were misinterpreted. For instance, an ad campaign which stressed that Blondie was the band was misinterpreted to mean that Harry was the sole focus of the band and that none of the other band members mattered. After a protracted period of frustration, they eventually gave up and got on with the job of making music instead.

Although future albums yielded up additional hits — including experiments in reggae and an early venrture into rap with the 1981 hit *Rapture* — Blondie never quite again captured the public's attention the way they had in 1978-79. With the slackening interest, the band members began eyeing outside projects. By 1982, Harry had decided to go solo and Blondie had split up by the end of the year.

For a time, Debbie Harry continued working in music, along with appearances in films and theater, but when Stein became seriously ill, Harry took time off to help him through his illness. Harry didn't disappear completely or for long, however. By 1986 she had released her second solo album, ROCKBIRD, which featured the great UK top 10 single, *French Kissin' (in the USA)*. She continued to put out new material through the 1980's and 1990's, also appearing in films and on television, but the popularity of her iconic past was never recaptured.

And perhaps it's just as well. The focus of Harry's work has become less about the look of the singer — an image that she portrayed only in order to be a part of a very dynamic and visual musical movement, — and more about her music and singing. The end of the 1990's saw Blondie get back together for an album, a tour and a live album. It was a stronger Debbie Harry who returned to the band than the new wave singer of the past. It's a change that suits her perfectly.

Selected Studio Albums (as part of Blondie):
- BLONDIE (Chrysalis, 1976, reissue)
- PLASTIC LETTERS (Chrysalis, 1977)
- PARALLEL LINES (Chrysalis, 1978)
- EAT TO THE BEAT (Chrysalis, 1979)
- AUTOAMERICAN (Chrysalis, 1980)
- THE HUNTER (Chrysalis, 1982)
- NO EXIT (EMI, 1999)

Selected Studio Albums:
- KOOKOO (Chrysalis, 1981)
- ROCKBIRD (Geffen, 1986)
- DEF, DUMB & BLONDE (Sire, 1989)
- DEBRAVATION (Sire, 1993)

Best of the "Best Of" Albums:
- THE BEST OF BLONDIE (Chrysalis, 1981)
- PLATINUM COLLECTION (EMI, 1994)

Live Albums:
  ∘ LIVE IN PHILADELPHIA 1978 / DALLAS 1980 (EMI, 1999)

~ 21 ~
Chrissie Hynde

While Debbie Harry and Blondie were stirring up the new wave movement on the New York side of the fence during the mid- to late-1970's, Ohio born Chrissie Hynde was doing the same in the UK thanks to her dedication to her band, The Pretenders. Hynde had also seen the birth of the punk movement in the 1970's and the progression of the music styles that changed rock music throughout the 1980's. More importantly, she continued to make music with her band, never stopping, long after other bands had come, gone, and reunited ten or twenty years down the line.

For any performer to keep a steady rock career going is one thing, for a women to do so in the male-dominated world of punk and new wave of the 1970's, it is amazing. Certainly it's one of the reasons why Hynde tends to be put on a pedestal by other women rockers today.

Born September 7, 1951 in Akron, Ohio, Hynde was already playing guitar in bands by the age of 16. After attending three years of art studies at Kent State University, she moved to London in 1973 and began writing album reviews for the New Musical Express magazine. In addition to writing about music, Hynde also began performing again and getting to know many of the people who would become linked to the punk movement within the next couple of years. Still, it wasn't until 1978 (and after relocating to Paris, then Cleveland, Ohio,

courtesy Hot Wacks

before returning to London) that she would put together the band that would become the Pretenders.

The Pretenders began as a traveling band and had a series of hit singles on the charts before their first album was released in 1980. Surprisingly, the album became a smash in the US (a market that, at that time, typically took an album or two to warm up to a new artist) besides hitting No. 1 in the UK. PRETENDERS was followed by a successful second release, PRETENDERS II, the band continuing with a sound that was a bright departure from the punk and new wave sound most listeners were accustomed to by that time. While new wave had moved to a more keyboard-oriented and bare guitar sound, Hynde's musical styles had a pop-oriented lyrical quality that was tempered with a strong rock beat and solid melodies. It also avoided the reliance on keyboards that so much of the new wave movement seemed tied to as the 1980's progressed. Meanwhile, Hynde's lyrics were certainly challenging, refusing to fall into an eternal cycle of love songs, as was the case with so many other artists.

By 1982 the The Pretenders were beginning to suffer the troubles of internal conflicts, particularly with the death of guitarist James Honeyman-Scott and the firing of Peter Farndon (who then passed away within the year). For most bands, losing one-half of the band would be enough to make them call it quits, but not Chrissie Hynde, who added new musicians and carried on.

courtesy Hot Wacks

The remainder of the 1980's saw Hynde release a series of albums under The Pretenders name, with many of them doing quite well on the charts. In fact, the downside of her continuous career is that there are hardly any true valleys in her career. Instead of faltering in some manner fighting the usual demons of the rock world, Hynde has continued to put out music that dose well on the charts. So there's been no great "back to basics" or "return to the public eye" as with performers who disappeared for a time and then had success with a "comeback." For an intelligent and serious musician like Hynde, there was never any need for a comeback — she's always been with us.

And I think most fans will agree that we've benefited from having Chrissie Hynde and her music around all this time. By remaining true to her goal — creating good music — Hynde has shown that longevity is not, like nostalgia, an intangible thing of the mind, but rather the vehicle by which a true artist displays an amazing and memorable career.

Selected Studio Albums:
- PRETENDERS (Sire, 1980)
- PRETENDERS II (Sire, 1981)
- LEARNING TO CRAWL (Sire, 1984)
- GET CLOSE (Sire, 1986)
- PACKED! (Sire, 1990)

- LAST OF THE INDEPENDENTS (Sire, 1994)
- VIVA EL AMOR (Warner Brothers, 1999)

Best of the "Best Of" Albums:
- THE SINGLES (Sire, 1987)

Live Albums:
- ISLE OF VIEW (Warner Brothers, 1995)

~ 22 ~
Etta James

There were a lot of contributors to the origins of the rock beat in the late 1940's and 50's. Some came from the country side of the fence, others from R&B. Either way, most found themselves thrust into the spotlight of the emerging sound that would soon become Rock and Roll.

That was the good side of rock's history. The bad side involves just how so many of these early rock heroes ended up being cast aside in the years that followed — some by their own hands, through drink and/or drugs, and others by the changing likes of the fickle public. In many cases, it was years before acknowledgements would be made to their contributions and in many cases it was too late.

Fortunately, it was not too late in coming for Etta James. Yet, along the way it was a strange and dark trip.

Born Jamesetta Hawkins on January 25, 1938 in Los Angeles, California, Etta showed a remarkable singing talent at a very early age. Having already sung in her church's choir by the age of five, she was singing in a girl group trio by the time she was 12 — singing so well, in fact, that in 1950-51 they were already performing in and around the San Francisco area. Of course, they saw it all simply as a chance to sing in front of an audience and hang out with older people in places that young girls definitely shouldn't be hanging out.

Looking to do some original material, Etta had the idea of doing a singing response to a popular hit at the time, the rocking *Work with Me Annie* by Hank Ballard and the Midnighters. Her song, *Roll with Me Henry*, began gaining local popularity, and when band leader Johnny Otis was told about the trio and their song, he wanted to hear them sing. Figuring the invitation was just a come-on to meet a group of young girls, Etta at first refused to do the tryout, but after being pressured by the other girls she went and Otis was pleased with the result.

They went with Otis to Los Angeles, where the trio was recorded with Etta as the vocalist and the other girls pushed to the background as The Peaches. Johnny Otis is

credited with shortening Jamesetta Hawkins to Etta James, the name that she would use from that time forward. *Roll with Me Henry* became an underground hit (sometimes retitled *The Wallflower* to avoid possible sexual connotations). The song was later covered by another artist under the "cleaner" title of *Dance with Me Henry* and made it into the hit parade. From there, Etta's claim to Rock and Roll roots — because of the rocking nature of her music and the suggestive lyrics — was pretty much assured.

After the song's release, Etta began playing clubs around the country and recording for Modern records, during which time she recorded another early rocker, *Good Rockin' Daddy*.

But it was with her move to Chess Records that Etta really began to leave her mark on music. Although usually constrained to singing ballads at Chess, Etta was also able to record a number of swinging and rocking tunes for the label over the years, including *Tell Mama* (which a young fan by the name of Janis Joplin later adopted for her own singing career).

In the 1970's, however, Etta hit on hard times, a dependency on drugs keeping her away from her singing. Still, even then, there was rarely a period where Etta wasn't recording, and even on her worst days she was pumping out music that many singers would have given their right arm to be able to match. Because of her absolute dedication to her music, although Etta may have left the limelight for a time, she was never very far from view.

In the 1980's, when looking back at the early days of rock music was in vogue, and Etta's name was one of the first to roll off people's tongues. This was the attention that Etta's career needed, and she shed the dependency that had kept her down for so long, and her career began to take off once again. Still recording and still managing to shift from jazz to rock without missing a beat, Etta is an example of a pioneer who's stood the test of time — physically and professionally — long enough to become a living legend.

Selected Solo Albums:
- MISS ETTA JAMES (Crown, 1961)
- AT LAST (Chess, 1961)
- CALL NY NAME (Cadet, 1966)
- TELL MAMA (Chess, 1968)
- ETTA IS BETTA THAN EVAH (Chess, 1978)
- DEEP IN THE NIGHT (Bullseye Blues, 1978)
- HICKORY DICKORY DOCK (Ace, 1998)
- THE HEART OF A WOMAN (Private Music, 1999)

Best of the "Best Of" Albums:
- THE BEST OF ETTA JAMES (JCI, 1972)
- HER GRESTEST SIDES, VOL. I (Chess, 1983)
- THE SWEETEST PEACHES / CHESS YEARS (Chess, 1988)
- THE ESSENTIAL ETTA JAMES (Chess, 1994)
- HER BEST (Chess, 1997)

Selected Live Albums:
- ROCKS THE HOUSE (Chess, 1964)
- ETTA: RED HOT 'N; LIVE (Intermedia, 1982)
- LIVE FROM SAN FRANCISCO (On The Spot, 1994)

~ 23 ~
Joan Jett

A persistent element throughout this book, one that applies to female and male performers alike, is "persona." When an artist or group successfully centers their early work on a particular image or persona, it becomes almost impossible to break free of that image. Almost inevitably a band or performer is stuck with that early image (rebel, a balladeer, punk act, whatever) and can never shake free of it because that image alone defines what the listening public expects them to be, and the dear people won't accept anything else. So all too often, if a career is allowed to continue it's its continuance is only in the form of a nostalgia act — endlessly repeating thirty year old hits, over and over, for ever, period. And anything pales with time.

But there are those who're able to break free of the early persona and go in new directions. Typically, when a performer does manage to break with the past, she'll at first refuse to look at her early days, concentrating strictly on perpetuating a new persona. Also typically, however, she'll eventually realize that the earlier material was every bit as good (maybe even better) than the newer stuff and will derive satisfaction (for audience and performer alike) in combining the old and the new in performance.

Joan Jett fits into another category altogether.

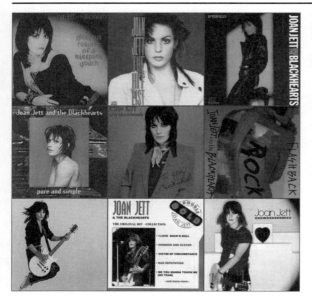

Born September 22, 1960 in Philadelphia, Pennsylvania, Joan found herself moving to Los Angeles when she was 12. By that time she was already interested in playing the guitar and performing music, so much so that she was already forming her own bands. In fact, it was her band, at the age of 15 that caught the eye of producer Kim Fowley, who was looking for an all girl group to rival the success of Suzi Quatro. Signing with Fowley, the band became The Runaways, and success in Europe and Japan wasn't long in coming.

As described in the entry for Lita Ford above, The Runaways began running out of steam by 1977, and in 1979 they broke up, although Fowley and the record label continued releasing the band's material for years using earlier recordings. The final split came about as a result of Lita Ford and Joan Jett wanting the band to move in very different directions: Lita towards the heavy metal sound that was just beginning to emerge again in the late 1970's, and Joan towards a faster paced Ramones-like sound that the punk movement was perpetuating, also in the late 70's. With no agreement in sight, Ford left the band and Jett continue under The Runaways's name for a briefly before going solo in 1979.

After spending some time recording with Paul Cook and Steve Jones of the Sex Pistols, Jett decided to go for a more straight forward rock sound and by August 1980 had formed her new band, The Blackhearts. Working with producer Kenny Laguna, Jett recorded her first solo album in 1980, but couldn't find a record label interested in an album featuring music that didn't fit in with the then-current popular genres. At that time, new wave was making a big splash and the disco days were drawing to a sputtering close. Most of the big name bands were recording music that was either experimental or based on heavily orchestrated productions, hoping to find an audience at a time when there were no clear musical directions in sight. Then along came Joan Jett with an album that was just good old fashion Rock and Roll. The labels figured it didn't stand a chance.

Frustrated at the lack of interest, Laguna released the album himself, with Ariola Records finally picking it up for distribution in Europe. It was enough to spark interest in Jett, and by January 1981, Neil Bogart (who had just left Casablanca to start his new label Boardwalk) had signed Jett and the band to a deal. The album was renamed BAD REPUTATION and reach No. 51 in the US — a good beginning for a performer who less than a year before had had no takers whatever.

Since the first album did well, there was definite interest in doing a second one. Joan made no attempt to change the musical direction of her earlier album, instead the second album was another collection of straight ahead, hard rocking new songs mixed with a few cover songs, and was released in March 1982 as I LOVE ROCK 'N' ROLL. The first single, the title song from the album, became a smash in the US, reaching No. 2. In a complete chart twist from the usual, the US was the country where success bloomed, with Joan doing amazingly well, while the UK charts saw her singles and albums alike only doing olny moderately well.

Joan followed *I Love Rock 'n' Roll* with two more singles from the same album, both of them cover songs: Tommy James' *Crimson and Clover* and Gary Glitter's *Do You Wanna Touch Me (Oh Yeah)*. Both became Top 20 hits in the US. In 1983 was the release of Joan's next album (this time on her own Blackheart label), called ALBUM, which featured two Top 40 singles, *Fake Friends* and the Sly Stone cover song, *Everyday People*.

By the time her next album, GLORIOUS RESULTS OF A MISSPENT YOUTH, was released in 1985, the interest in the US was beginning to fade. The album still hit No. 67 in the US, but in 1986 her next album, GOOD MUSIC, didn't even break the Top 100. Still, Jett refused to change her style and after a brief flirtation with acting (appearing in the 1987 film LIGHT OF DAY, which contained a Springsteen-written title single for Joan that hit No. 33), she came back with another album of hard rocking songs called UP YOUR ALLEY.

ALLEY returned her to the Top 20, with *I Hate Myself for Loving You* reaching No. 8 and *Little Liar* going to No. 19 on the charts. It was enough to convince Joan that her style of music may go in and out of fashion, but one way or another people usually came back around to it. Although her later albums haven't done as well on the charts, there's been no reason for Joan to consider changing her musical direction. Instead, she continues to perform live — and is certainly one of the hardest working women rockers when you consider how often she's performed live every year since the early 1980's — and continues to play the music that she wants to play.

Pin her as a Rock and Roller. Say that she's stuck on playing the same old thing again and again. It doesn't matter. She's playing what she loves and never had a reason to feel that it was a trap from which she need escape. If only more performers could have that kind of luck in their careers.

Selected Studio Albums (as part of the Runaways):
- ○ RUNAWAYS (Touchwood, 1976)
- ○ QUEENS OF NOISE (Touchwood, 1977)
- ○ WAITIN' FOR THE NIGHT (Mercury, 1977)
- ○ AND NOW THE RUNAWAYS (Cherry Red, 1980)
- ○ FLAMIN' SCHOOLGIRLS (Cherry Red, 1980)
- ○ LITTLE LOST GIRLS (Cherry Red, 1981)

    (It should be noted that only the first three albums were released during Joan Jett's time with the band. All other albums were released after the band had using material from earlier recording sessions.)

Selected Studio Albums (solo):
- ○ JOAN JETT (Ariola, 1980)
- ○ BAD REPUTATION (Blackheart, 1981 — this is essentially the same as the 1980 Ariola album)
- ○ I LOVE ROCK & ROLL (Blackheart, 1981)
- ○ ALBUM (Blackheart, 1983)
- ○ GLORIOUS RESULTS OF A MISSPENT YOUTH (Blackheart, 1984)
- ○ GOOD MUSIC (Epic, 1986)
- ○ UP YOUR ALLEY (Epic, 1988)
- ○ THE HIT LIST (Epic, 1990)
- ○ NOTORIOUS (Epic, 1991)
- ○ PURE AND SIMPLE (Warner Brothers, 1994)
- ○ FETISH (Blackheart, 1999)

Live Album (as part of the Runaways):
- ○ LIVE IN JAPAN (Mercury, 1977)

Best of the "Best Of" Albums:
- ○ FLASHBACK (Blackheart, 1994)
- ○ FIT TO BE TIED: GREAT HITS BY JOAN JETT (Mercury/Blackheart, 1997)
- ○ THE BEST OF THE RUNAWAYS (Mercury, 1987)

~ 24 ~
Janis Joplin

There was a book about the sleazy side of the rock business. What the title was and what the whole book was about are unimportant, the topic was all that mattered to people who picked it up. In the book were several photos of rock performers in various stages of arrest, death and other tragedies to highlight the terrible things that happened to people in the business, and one of those photos was Janis Joplin.

It was a dark black and white photo of a topless Janis, stretched out on a deserted beach, with a half emptied bottle in one hand, and a drunken slur on her lips. You could tell that it was taken at a time of drunken unawareness, and that it was now being used to simply sell the desperate image of Janis as a drunken loser of life.

Shocking and depressing, it fulfilled the role intended by the book, and that seems to have been Janis' station since before her death — fulfilling a role. Each generation has had its martyr — think of Marilyn Monroe, John Lennon, Elvis, Valentino . . . Onward these idols have climbed to some sort of sainthood — not because of what they did in life, but because of what tragically happened in their last moments, leaving people with unanswered questions. In death, Janis became a monument to the "live fast, die young" mythology that had become so prevalent in the Rock and Roll life style (sharing that role with Jim Morrison and Jimi Hendrix, whose similarly times deaths had the same impact). She also became a force for feminism, showing that women could be the main focus of a rock band, or be the headliner instead of just part of the band. She also became a symbol of loss, of mystery, of desperation. Some will always ask, why did she have to die then and there?

Yet, none of these things really deal with the person Janis was. All the books and documentaries give glimpses, but in trying to draw a bigger picture, they end up with a smaller message than what was really there.

Born January 19, 1943 in Port Arthur, Texas, Janis grew up singing. She had started when she was young, singing in bars and honky tonks because it was one of the few things in life that she felt comfortable doing, and she could feel the attention and appreciation of her audience. At first, she believed that singing was to be her career and moved out to San Francisco, California in 1964 in order to fulfill her dreams. Within two years, however, she had returned to Texas, afraid that the lifestyle she'd found in California, with such easy access booze and pills, would be her possible undoing.

While readying herself to go back to college and contemplating the possibility of marriage, she was offered an opportunity to return to California and sing with a rock band called Big Brother and the Holding Company. Although worried by could happen out there, Janis took the chance and began singing with the group, who went on to become the house band at the Avalon Ballroom. By the fall of 1966, Big Brother had been signed to a record deal, but the album they recorded did little to excite anyone and the

label, Mainstream, was reluctant to release the finished product.

So they continued plugging away, playing the ballroom and other clubs until the time of the Monterey Pop Festival in June 1967. It was at this moment that everything changed for the band, the music, and for Janis. After years of playing the bars, Janis had perfected her persona, a smoky, soul tortured singing voice and flamboyant stage moves that perfectly matched the heartbreaking, soulful music of Big Brother. These elements combined with entering the spotlight at a festival concert that was a showcase for many extraordinary talents, Janis and Big Brother left everyone with their jaws dropping and gasping for breath.

Word got around quickly that Big Brother was a band to see, and especially their volatile singer. In 1968, CBS recognized the opportunity to sign another promising rock seller on their label and bought the band's contract from Mainstream. Big Brother then recorded the album that was to become their pinnacle, as well as Janis Joplin's — CHEAP THRILLS. The album included three tracks would become those most strongly associated with Janis' memory for many fans — *Summertime*, *Piece of My Heart* and *Ball & Chain*. The album reached No. 1 in the US and the band was assured of success.

Then, of course, things changed. By December of 1968, Janis had been convinced that she had to work outside the band, that they were holding her back. She was now going to be a solo artist who didn't need hangers-on, like a band, any more. It was going to be Janis alone that brought people in, because that's what people were saying anyhow.

Moving to a more soul oriented sound, Janis invested time in building a new band around her called the Kozmic Blues Band. They released one album, I GOT DEM OL' KOZMIC BLUES AGAIN MAMA!, and spent a year touring before they disbanded. For many, the album was acceptable (and it did reach No. 5 in the US), but it didn't really seem to show the Janis that people thought they knew from her earlier work.

Realizing that a bigger rock and perhaps even a country feel was probably closer to her roots than the soul sound, Janis got back together a couple of times with Big Brother in 1970. Mostly, however, she spent her time putting together another band called the Full-Tilt Boogie Band. It was with this band that she began to record her next album, PEARL, when she passed away from a heroin overdose on October 4, 1970.

For most careers that would have been the end. But the tortured soul of the singer had impressed upon people the idea that there had to be more to find out, more to hear, than what was already there. Understandable as well — after all, Janis had really only recorded three albums in her lifetime that were released, and many saw the Mainstream Big Brother album as not being sufficient evidence on which to pass judgement because its questionable quality.

So PEARL was released. It was No. 1 for nine weeks and made *Me and Bobby McGee* a major hit, even though it sounded like nothing she'd done before and was in no way reminiscent of the bite that she'd always projected in her music. It didn't matter though, because the singer had gone to her rest and was safely locked away so that one could praise her without worrying about how she might screw up her career. It was safe now. She could be molded into what people wanted to believe.

So people came out of the woodwork and began telling their stories. Some provided elements of truth about the life that Janis had led, but most didn't want to hear it. Others talked about how manly she was, or how feminine her singing was. Former lovers paraded up and down, each exclaiming that nobody knew her he they did, claiming a special role in her life, when, in fact, they really had no idea what Janis was all about either.

So more albums come out. More tributes. More stories. But in building up the goddess, they've all forgotten about the person that their musings are based on — the singer who just wanted to sing songs and get people moving. She didn't care about being a symbol, she wanted to pour something out of her soul in a way that people could see and hear. If she could see what people had done to her over the years, she'd probably shudder and wonder what had gone wrong.

There's another photo of Janis. One that was taken of her sometime before her death. A photo of her standing naked with a dark background, light filtering on to her face and body, several necklaces around her neck. In her eyes, which reach out to the camera, you can see a person that was looking for something. Looking for acceptance. Looking for life. Looking for a chance to say something and not be cut down for it.

It was a picture of flickering hope. A picture of sharing. It was something that people never gave her, and still don't quite understand to this day.

Selected Studio Albums (as part of Big Brother and the Holding Company):
  ○ BIG BROTHER & THE HOLDING COMPANY (Mainstream, 1967)
  ○ CHEAP THRILLS (Columbia, 1968)

Selected Studio Albums:
  ○ I GOT DEM OL' KOZMIC BLUES AGAIN MAMA! (Columbia, 1969)
  ○ PEARL (Columbia, 1971)

Best of the "Best Of" Albums:
- GREATEST HITS (Columbia, 1973)
- BOX OF PEARLS (Sony, 1999)

~ 25 ~
Chaka Khan

The early 1970's was a unique time for rock music. With a wide variety of music hitting rock radio, it allowed artists to cross over between genres who otherwise would have been banging their heads against the wall, and not being heard. That had changed by the late 70's, and many of those same artists soon found that radio could be very fickle, and could leave them hanging as definitions of what constituted Rock and Roll music were continuously changing.

So, the early 70's allowed new artists to be heard who showed that their particular styles of rock could be commercially successful. And it also allowed certain voices to be heard that subsequently helped shape singing styles for years to come. Chaka Khan was one of those voices. Hers was and remains one of the best voices of the funk and rock movement.

Born Yvette Stevens on March 23, 1953 in Chicago, Illinois, Chaka found herself going in two directions while growing up. On one hand, she had become involved with the Black Panthers (where she adopted the name she goes by today) and working in their breakfast program, while on the other hand she was performing in a girl group called the Crystalettes that played around the area. By the time she was 16, she had decided that rock music was going to be her answer and ran away from home to find that answer.

She joined a band called Lyfe in 1969 as a singer, then moved on to another band called the Babysitters by 1972. It was there that she met up with Kevin Murphy and Andre Fisher, with whom she formed the band Rufus. Rufus was the band that brought Chaka national attention, their music fitting quite nicely into the strong mix of funk and soul being played on rock music radio at the time. With her strong and energetic vocals, it wasn't long before other artists began praising her singing abilities. In 1978 Khan went solo and found success with the single *I'm Every Woman*, but she was still legally bound to Rufus, who were unhappy about the competition, but were willing to promote themselves as Rufus, featuring Chaka Khan.

Khan continued to work with Rufus and on solo material for the next few years, but the albums weren't selling as well at they had in the mid-1970's. That changed, however, with the release of her 1984 album I FEEL FOR YOU. The album's first single, a cover of a Prince song and the title track of the album, was a Top 20 hit in both the UK and the US. It was enough to revitalize her career to the point of confirming her place as one of the greatest ever funk / rock singers, and she continued to prove that with a series of albums in the 1980's.

By 1990, Khan had realized that styles were changing, but was disappointed when the record labels felt that she had to be promoted as a dance music artist. Fed up with being chained to an image she felt didn't suit her, Chaka relocated to Europe she could be much more diverse with her material than she could be in the US.

Still working in music, Chaka Khan still thrills audiences with a voice that crosses many genre boundaries at will without ever being anything but her own.

Selected Studio Albums (as part of Rufus):
- RUFUS (ABC, 1973)
- RAGS TO RUFUS (ABC, 1974)
- RUFUSIZED (ABC, 1975)
- RUFUS FEATURING CHAKA KHAN (ABC, 1975)
- ASK RUFUS (ABC, 1977)
- STREET PLAYER (ABC, 1978)
- MASTERJAM (MCA, 1979)
- CAMOFLAGE (MCA, 1981)

Selected Studio Albums:
- CHAKA (Warner Brothers, 1978)
- NAUGHTY (Warner Brothers, 1980)
- WHAT CHA' GONNA DO FOR ME (Warner Brothers, 1981)
- CHAKA KHAN (Warner Brothers, 1982)
- I FEEL FOR YOU (Warner Brothers, 1984)
- DESTINY (Warner Brothers, 1987)
- C.K. (Warner Brothers, 1989)
- LIFE IS A DANCE (Warner Brothers, 1989)
- THIS WOMAN I AM (Warner Brothers, 1992)
- COME 2 MY HOUSE (New Power Generation, 1998)

Live Albums:
- RUFUS AND CHAKA KHAN LIVE: STOMPIN AT THE SAVOY (Warner Brothers, 1983)

Best of the "Best Of" Albums:
  ◦ EPIPHANY: THE BEST OF CHAKA KHAN (Warner Brothers, 1996)
  ◦ I'M EVERY WOMAN (Warner Brothers, 1999)

~ 26 ~
Carole King

Every once in a while, a genuine artist enters the music business as a songwriter. For some, a songwriting career is exactly what they want and they excel at supplying a variety of performers with recording material formany years. Others, however, want a bit more out of life than just supplying others with songs — they want the chance to perform their songs themselves in front of an audience. Some songwriters are able to make the leap from their behind-the-scenes role to being the main attraction on stage. This has been the case for some big name peformers, like Neil Sedaka and Neil Diamond, and it's certainly been the case for Carole King.

Born Carole Klein in Brooklyn, New York on February 9, 1942, Carole learned the piano at the age of four and was already forming her own bands by the time she was in high school. It was in college that she found a professional connection to Rock and Roll music when she met up with a few guys at Queens College who were struggling to make it as songwriters: Neil Sedaka, Paul Simon and Gerry Goffin.

Working with Goffin (whom she would later marry), King began writing material for Aldon Music, based out of the Brill Building. One of the owners of Aldon Music, Don Kirshner, liked Carole's voice and offered her a chance to record some singles, just as Neil Sedaka had done previously with his successful hit *Oh! Carol*, a song written about King. None of the three singles done by King hit the charts (although a later song *It Might As Well Rain Until September* did well in 1962), but it mattered little as the Goffin-King writing team soon struck gold with *Will You Love Me Tomorrow*. That song, recorded by the Shirelles in 1961, hit No. 1 and was closely followed by a No. 9 hit for the Drifters written by the Goffin-King team, *Up on the Roof.*

For the next several years, the Goffin-King connection could be depended on to write dozens of hit songs for a variety of artists that came to the Brill Building. Success as performers seemed to be out of their reach, and King in particular wanting to do more recording of her own. By 1967 the marriage was over, although the two stayed together long enough to form a short lived label, Tomorrow Records, that recorded another single for King called *Some of Your Lovin'* (a cover of an earlier hit for Dusty Springfield). Moving to Los Angeles in 1968, King formed a band with her second husband Charles Larkey and with Danny Kortchmar called The City. They recorded one album for Ode Records, but the album stiffed with no touring to support it. King, as it turned out, had been quite reluctant to perform live and this, along with the album's low sales, soon caused the band to break up.

Lou Adler, the producer of the album, was still interested in King, however. Her first solo album, WRITER, was released in early 1970 to little fanfare, but that didn't deter Adler and King from working together on a follow-up. The second album, TAPESTRY, was the one that brought Carole King out as a major performer once and for all.

TAPESTRY stayed on the charts for an amazing six years and was one of the best selling rock albums of the 1970's. It also showcased a number of hit singles, including *It's Too Late*, *So Far Away* and *I Feel the Earth Move*. King followed up with MUSIC in 1971, RHYMES AND REASONS in 1972 and WRAP AROUND JOY in 1974. All three hit the Top 10 and produced Top 10 singles (two of which reached No. 1).

There's no denying the fact that Carole King was a major rock performer in the 1970's. She followed up her albums of the early 70's with several more, but after 1983 began to distance herself from the music world. This was partly because of changes in the recording industry that didn't sit well with her, but mostly because of her hesitance at performing publicly. She moved to Idaho and became involved in the environmental movement. Eventually she returned to music with her album CITY STREETS in 1989, followed by COLOR OF YOUR DREAMS in 1993. Since then, she's made occasional appearances on television and in public performances, but she's felt little need to prove anything more to herself. The hit songs that she for herself and for others far outweigh what most other songwriters have ever been able to accomplish in the rock music field, and her legacy as a major contributor to Rock and Roll is assured.

Selected Studio Albums:
- WRITER (Epic, 1970)
- TAPESTRY (Epic, 1971)
- MUSIC (Epic, 1971)
- RHYMES AND REASONS (Epic, 1972)
- FANTASY (Epic, 1973)
- WRAP AROUND JOY (Epic, 1974)
- REALLY ROSIE (Epic, 1975)

- ○ THOROUGHBRED (Epic, 1976)
- ○ SIMPLE THINGS (Capitol, 1977)
- ○ WELCOME HOME (Capitol, 1978)
- ○ TOUCH THE SKY 1979 (Capitol, 1979)
- ○ PEARLS (Capitol, 1980)
- ○ ONE TO ONE (Atlantic, 1982)
- ○ SPEEDING TIME (Atlantic, 1983)
- ○ CITY STREETS (Capitol, 1989)
- ○ COLOR OF YOUR DREAMS (Rhythm Safari, 1993)

Best of the "Best Of" Albums:
- ○ HER GREATEST HITS (Epic, 1978)
- ○ SUPER HITS (Sony, 2000)

Live Albums:
- ○ IN CONCERT (Rhythm Safari, 1994)
- ○ CARNEGIE HALL CONCERT: JUNE 18, 1971 (Sony, 1996)

~ 27 ~
Cyndi Lauper

It was a moment that sent chills down the spine. A moment that came so early in her career that it seems to been half forgotten by all but the most devoted of fans.

It was 1980 and a band called Blue Angel was recording a music video for their second single, a cover of the Gene Pitney hit *I'm Gonna Be Strong*. In the video, the female lead singer begins the vocals on top of a piano in a shy and timid emotional state. Then, as the song continues, with the thoughts of a shattered soul who refuses to show heartbreak in front of her ex-lover, the vocals become stronger. As the music continues, the singer moves to the center of the stage where the rest of the band performs, emerging from the song only long enough to pound the air as the drums ricochet between choruses. Finally, the song comes to a climax with the girl admitting that once the guy is gone, she'll finally break down and cry. The emotion in the singer's voice, and the look on her face say exactly what so many have faced in such a real life situation.

Yet, that's not the moment that really startles.

That comes next. The singer repeats the final word again — "Cry." It's stronger than before and comes forcefully from her small frame. Then the word comes once again, louder and with a surge of physical energy even more intense. Finally, she forces the word out one more time. And it's at this point that it's no longer Cyndi Lauper forming the word and reaching the back of the hall with the sound; it's as if the word, the sound, the voice itself has taken over her entire body and held her momentarily in its grasp. Her body bounds backwards quickly, as her eyes grow wide and when she moves forward to sing that final note, it's a moment of sheer clarity that shatters the nature of the song from an ironic twist of fate and emotion, to a desperate shout in the lonely night.

It was a voice that stood out in the darkness.

It was a voice that Cyndi Lauper nearly destroyed as well.

Born Cynthia Ann Stephanie Lauper on June 22, 1952, Cyndi first lived in Brooklyn, New York. After her parents divorced when Cyndi was five, her mother moved Cyndi and her siblings to Ozone Park, still in New York City. As she got older, schooling did little to help Cyndi embrace the normality of the world around her, and she found herself going from school to school until leaving home at the age of 17.

The only element of her life about which she felt strongly, other than her family, was singing. Performing show tunes for the old women in the neighborhood at an early age, and getting paid for it, made Cyndi realize that she had a talent that no one could take away from her (or put her down for). When she left home, she traveled Canada for a year before returning to Ozone Park, still aching to be more than just a normal person — the ones that had always looked at her oddly anyway — and still wanting to show that she could be something on her own.

Struggling, Cyndi began singing on street corners and finally progressed to working as a lead singer in 1974 with the group Doc West. Although strictly a cover band (playing only hit songs by other artists) with a strong leaning towards disco, they gained a small following in the New York area. Performing with the band, Cyndi was becoming known as a singer who could mimic other vocal styles in a flash, including what was reported to be a stunning transformation into Janis Joplin for a portion of their set every night.

Unfortunately, like most bands struggling by doing covers, they eventually broke up. Cyndi soon found another band, this one called Flyer, to work with. While the new band allowed her to get away from doing disco, it was still just another cover band. So even though they was playing gigs in better establishments, it was still a stagnant creative situation for the musicians involved.

It also led to Cyndi tearing up her voice to the point where she had trouble speaking, let alone singing. Although she could sing up a storm, she had never been trained to use her voice properly and through extensive misuse had damaged it almost beyond repair. It was now 1977 and Cyndi was no closer to having a career based solely on her singing than she had been when she first left home. In fact, it was beginning to look like she never would.

Although the doctors that she'd seen felt that the prognosis was poor, Cyndi turned to voice coach Katie Agestra and spent most of the following year working on regaining her vocal abilities and increasing her singing ability. By 1978, Cyndi was back to performing, but without a band — Flyer having moved on with another singer — and Cyndi became a solo artist once again.

A meeting with musician John Turi in 1978 led to the formation of a new band called Blue Angel. This band was a unique mixture of pop, girl group, rockabilly, and even a dash of hard rock on occasions. More importantly, it was a group that created its own music, and although an occasional cover song would enter a set, it was mostly new music. It was also exciting, with the mixture of styles making the band a unique act on the club scene.

Which was the problem. It was too unique, too different. The rockabilly revival by acts like The Stray Cats and Steve Forbit was still a couple of years off. 1978-79 was a time when a band had to be punk, disco, soul or pop. Musical forms had become quite rigid, no at all embracing variety, and Blue Angel had difficulty finding appreciative audiences in the rock world. Once again, being different from the norm made Cyndi stand out, but the world simply staring at her, as if at an oddball.

Blue Angel landed a record deal with Polydor in 1979 for two albums, their self-titled first of which was released in 1980. It was then that two early music videos were done, one for the aforementioned *I'm Gonna Be Strong* and their first single *I Had a Love*. There was mention of the band in Rolling Stone and several other magazines, and many critics favorably reviewed the album.

But it went nowhere. Following the album's poor performance, the band began to split apart, accompanied by disagreements with the label and their manager, so they broke up in 1982. Polydor never pursued the promised follow-up album and Cyndi once again found herself adrift.

She was, once again, back to simply making ends meet (working as a singer in a Japanese bar in Manhattan) and still attending voice lessons with Katie Agestra. In trying to get her career back on track, Cyndi worked with Rick Derringer on some demos, and spent time searching for a new manager. In 1983 she found David Wolff, a manager who was interested in Cyndi's work, and had also been working with the CBS label, Portrait Records, with his band Arc Angel. With Wolff's help, Cyndi recorded her first solo album during the spring and summer of 1983.

The album was SHE'S SO UNUSUAL. It was to be become one of the most successful albums of the 1980's and the first album to achieve four Top 5 singles from a debut album by a female performer. *Girls Just Want To Have Fun* was the first single from the album and the first music video. Both presented Cyndi in a way that was far from the norm for a female rock performer at the time. In 1983-84, the world was still coming back from the punk / new-wave / disco era where female singers had to look like divas, fantasy mystery women or street punks. Cyndi was none of those in the video or in person. Nor was her music easily adapted to any of these formulas. Her music was neither the music of a temptress, nor the pining love song so popular with female artists at the time. It was a person's voice coming through, and the songs very much reflected Cyndi's personal viewpoint — she wasn't setting out to seduce anyone or yell at them, she just wanted to get up, sing and have fun. The songs dealt with being a girl and still having fun (as in the first single), the demands in one's life that put strain on love (*Time After Time*), the ironies of fame (*Money Changes Everything*) and even the rarely touched upon subject of female self-gratification (*She-Bop*). More importantly, the album rocked, and letting it run through a few times without a break was good fun. It was different from anything else that was out there. She really was so unusual.

Her personality came through in her looks as well. By this time her hair was a blazing red that had been hacked off on the right side of her head (and later complimented by a checkered design in her scalp). Her clothes were not the designer-wear of other female performers, but mix-and-match skirts, tops, jackets, hats, bangles, scarves, necklaces and jewelry that would have sent a fashion expert shrieking into the night. It was also obvious that at times Cyndi was exaggerating her speaking voice in order to give it an almost unworldly, cartoon-like flavor by way of Brooklyn (it was only in moments of serious discussions during interviews that Cyndi's voice would return to normal in those early days of stardom).

She was everything you did NOT expected from a pop-star. And for once Cyndi was not being look upon as an outcast, but rather as a leader. Her look, her speaking voice, and her tongue-in-cheek humor all played hand-in-hand with her musical message of being an independent and thinking woman. Being so fresh and different, people, of course, wanted to know more about her.

It was reflected not only in the sales of Cyndi's first solo album, but also in the awards that came afterward. The Grammy people picked Cyndi as Best New Artist in 1984 (with her album art picking up an award as well), while the first MTV Video Music Awards honored her with Best Female Video. The American Music Awards voted Cyndi Best Female Pop Artist and awarded her Best Female Pop Song (*Time After Time*). By October 1984 the album had gone Double Platinum and the first three singles all went Gold by 1989. All this just in the US alone.

One aspect of her career that appeared with the first video was a bizarre association with the world of wrestling. Having Captain Lou Albano (a former wrestler still working in the field as a manager at the time) starring as her Dad in the *Girls Just Wanna Have Fun* video was just the first step. Then Cyndi began appearing at wrestling events and a whole phenomena called "Rock N' Wrestling" was happening which involved several rock performers getting involved with wrestling on a grand scale (and the WWF wrestling league even going so far to produce a rock album — with Cyndi making an appearance under a fake name).

At first, it was an interesting idea that grew into a sluggish snowball and left some fans cold. The pinnacle of the wrestling connection came with the release of the video for *The Goonies 'R' Good Enough*, a track that Cyndi did by for the soundtrack album of the Steven Spielberg produced film THE GOONIES. It was a nice song, but Cyndi's persona had by now become almost cartoonish, the humor of the music and the performer lost in the exaggerated world of wrestling. It was soon after that the wrestling connection was left behind for good, as Cyndi worked on her second album.

In 1986, with the release of TRUE COLORS, her second solo album, she must have felt it was time for a change. Besides co-producing the album, Cyndi co-wrote many of the tracks and the album's theme is more subdued than SHE'S SO UNUSUAL. TRUE COLORS went Platinum by November 1986 and featured two Top 5 hits (*True Colors* and *Change of Heart*) and had a Top 20 hit with *What's Going On*. Yet the album didn't receive the awards that the previous one had.

Which was fine with Cyndi, it seems. It was more to do with the music than the persona or the glamour. She would leave even more of it behind with her next album in 1989, A NIGHT TO REMEMBER, a serious theme-related album about the difficulties of love and the struggle of finding someone. Cyndi had also taken on the mantle of video director by this point and started creating her own vision of what the videos could be rather than just the usual MTV staple "concert footage" that seemed to be the normal fare for most performers. She also moved on from David Wolff's management around this time as well.

Although her subsequent albums never recreated the phenomenal sales success of SHE'S SO UNUSUAL, they were greater creative successes, especially the 1991 album HAT FULL OF STARS. 1994 saw the release of a "best of" collection called TWELVE DEADLY CYNS ...AND THEN SOME, which was released simultaneously with a video cassette of many of her videos. Cyndi continued to perform and record, releasing a new album in 1996 called SISTERS OF AVALON, another progressive step, followed in 1998 with a Christmas album called MERRY CHRISTMAS ... HAVE A NICE LIFE.

And this wasn't all, either. There were several movie appearances (including the hardly seen, yet very funny film VIBES), guest appearances on other albums, and a recurring guest role on the comedy series MAD ABOUT YOU (leading to an Emmy Award in 1995). All in all, she did things it the way she saw fit and never once changed to suit what people expected of her. She's followed faithfully what she expected of herself.

Her influence to the world of rock music comes with the message that women rockers don't have to pretend to be either ultra-serious or ultra-sexual. Nor was there any need to play yourself down to a lower level simply because it was expected of women on stage. And while many performers would have simply tried following up the first album with a "SHE'S SO UNUSUAL II," Cyndi was and is too serious an artist to have done so. Her albums have explored topics facing people in general and not just matters relating to women. While a sense of fun has always been maintained on her albums, war, spousal abuse, domestic difficulties, society's ills and more have all been dealt with in her songs. In conscientiously tackling the tough but important topics, Cyndi has reminded fans and fellow musicians that women can get up on stage and sing, have fun, and yet still have something important to say. And it's lead to some listeners taking a second look, and realizing that you don't have to take it seriously all the time. And if you don't, then when the message does become serious, it can have even more of an impact.

Cyndi stuck her foot in the door in the early 1980's, and through her popularity and her music, held that door open so that rock fans could peek inside and see beyond the usual flash and gender, and listen to what was worth hearing. Many other artists may have be in the spotlight for much longer than she was, but Cyndi Lauper's mark is already indelibly etched.

In being unusual, she ended up being a leader.

Selected Studio Albums (as part of Blue Angel):
  ○ BLUE ANGEL (Polydor, 1980; also reissued in 1984)

Selected Studio Albums:
  ○ SHE'S SO UNUSUAL (Epic, 1983)
  ○ TRUE COLORS (Epic, 1986)
  ○ A NIGHT TO REMEMBER (Epic, 1989)
  ○ HAT FULL OF STARS (Epic, 1993)
  ○ SISTERS OF AVALON (Epic, 1996)
  ○ MERRY CHRISTMAS . . . HAVE A NICE LIFE (Epic, 1998)

Best of the "Best Of" Albums:
  ○ TWELVE DEADLY CYNS . . . AND THEN SOME (Sony/Epic, 1994)

~ 28 ~
Brenda Lee

With the passage of time, we can sometimes forget those who were there at the beginning. And one of the most often forgotten women rockers is Brenda Lee. In the very early 1960's, Brenda was considered one of the hottest women in the Rock and Roll world — and certainly a leading star in the country branch of rock that transformed into rockabilly when Jerry Lee Lewis and Elvis were first starting out. She was also a teen idol, mainly because she was a teen herself. By 1960 she was an international sensation and other artists were trying hard to get her on their tours. Her career continued through the 1960's and into the 70's at which time her music began moving back towards her country roots.

When remembered today, people tend to think of Lee as being and having been strictly a country artist. A quick glimpse at her career shows that that's clearly not the case. So, what happened that changed people's perception?

Brenda Mae Tarpley was born on December 11, 1944 in Lithonia, Georgia to a working class family where both parents worked to make ends make. Brenda had become known in her neighborhood for her singing voice at a very early age, and she was also considered a prodigy in memorizing lyrics and song structure from just a couple of passes on the radio. At the age of seven, Brenda's father died during a construction site mishap and, in order to make ends met, Brenda's mother hit on the notion of Brenda's making a little cash for the family by singing at functions around the state.

By the time she was 11 (and had taken the stage name of Brenda Lee), she had already made a television appearance on OZARK JUBILEE, a program starring country performer Red Foley. Foley's manager, Dub Allbritton, was so taken by Brenda's singing that he became her personal manager and remained so until his death in 1972. By the time she was 12, she had appeared on several national television shows, including ED SULLIVAN and THE STEVE ALLEN SHOW. She'd also signed a deal with Decca Records, who released her first single, *Jambalaya*.

Building from that single, Brenda slowly became known for her powerhouse vocals, which were emphasized by her petite size and looks — she looked much younger than her age even at 13 and 14 years old. She also gained fame in Europe thanks to a booking at the Olympia in Paris, France where she was originally deemed too young to perform. When Allbritton went to the press with a phony story that Brenda was actually a thirty-year-old midget, the press went nuts. By the time the dust had settled (and Allbritton had refused to admit that he'd planted the story), the promoter of the show had to put Lee back into the program. She was held over for five weeks and became known in most of Europe because of the incident.

It was 1960 when Brenda broke into the Rock and Roll world. Although recording with Patsy Cline's producer, Owen Bradley, made many of Lee's songs sound much like Cline, Lee's preference was directed towards songs that had a more pop orientation, such as *Sweet Nothin'*, which hit No. 4 on the US charts. Her next song was probably her biggest ever hit, *I'm Sorry*, a song that went straight to No. 1.

While the music still had a country flavor to it, the songs also had a rock beat behind them and with her age being still a major factor in her favor (she was still only 16 when *Sweet Nothin'* and *I'm Sorry* hit the charts), she was considered one of the teenagers' own. In essence, she was the first true female teen idol of the early 1960's. Because of her popularity, she was asked to appear on many rock tours of the period, and to appear in films geared to the teen rockers. The hits kept coming as well, including *Emotions, Dum Dum, Fool No. 1* and *I Want to be Wanted.*

There was only one thing that happened that could change the focus of Brenda's career, and eventually it happened: she got older. By 1963 she had eloped, graduated from high school, and was no longer the teen idol who was on the same wavelength as other kids her age. It was also the time of the Beatles, and the teen idol fixation of the kids between 1958 and 1962 was definitely dwindling, being swallowed by the British Invasion and bands that wrote and recorded their own songs.

Brenda's career was far from over, though, and she continued having hits right through the 1960's. She also had continued popularity in Europe, where there had never been the teen idol factor Brenda that had sustantiated her popularity in the US. Europe was more interested in her singing voice than her status as a teenager. With the coming of the 1970's, Brenda's natural inclination was to return to a country sound, and that's where her career has been focused since 1973 and to the present.

It's clear that Brenda has no resentment of the changes that occurred in life as her career has moved along, and she still performs many of her hits to full houses when she tours. It's also likely that she clearly realizes she was the first of all the many women rockers who have become popular solo artists at an early age. She must know that she paved the way for all those who've come along since then. There's no heartache from her perspective over the passage of time, but my heart aches when those of us here today forget just how much she's given to us.

Selected Studio Albums:
- GRANDMA, WHAT GREAT SONGS YOU SANG (Decca, 1959)
- THIS IS ... BRENDA (Decca, 1960)
- BRENDA LEE (Decca, 1960)
- ALL THE WAY (Decca, 1961)
- MISS DYNAMITE (Brunswick, 1961)
- EMOTIONS (Decca, 1961)
- SINCERELY, BRENDA LEE (Decca, 1962)
- BRENDA, THAT'S ALL (Decca, 1962)
- ALL ALONE AM I (Decca, 1963)
- LET ME SING (Decca, 1964)
- MERRY CHRSTIMAS FROM BRENDA LEE (Decca, 1964)
- BY REQUEST (Decca, 1964)
- SONGS EVERYBODY KNOWS (Decca, 1964)
- THE ERSATILE BRENDA LEE (Decca, 1965)
- TOO MANY RIVERS (Decca, 1965)
- BYE BYE BLUES (Decca, 1966)
- COMING ON STRONG (Decca, 1966)
- REFLECTIONS IN BLUE (Decca, 1967)
- FOR THE FIRST TIME (Decca, 1968)
- CALL ME (MCA, 1968)

- ○ GOOD LIFE (MCA, 1968)
- ○ JOHNNY ONE TIME (Decca, 1969)
- ○ A WHOLE LOTTA (MCA, 1972)
- ○ BRENDA (MCA, 1973)
- ○ NEW SUNRISE (MCA, 1974)
- ○ NOW (MCA, 1975)
- ○ L.A. SESSIONS (MCA, 1977)

Best of the "Best Of" Albums:
- ○ LITTLE MISS DYNAMITE (MCA, 1980)
- ○ THE BRENDA LEE STORY — HER GREATEST HITS (MCA, 1974)
- ○ ANTHOLOGY VOLS. 1 & 2 (MCA, 1991)
- ○ LITTLE MISS DYNAMITE (Bear Family, 1997)

Live Albums:
- ○ LIVE DYNAMITE (Charly, 1997)

~ 29 ~
Annie Lennox

There was a period in the early 1980's when some rock performers experimented with an androgynous look. It wasn't the first time that visual uniqueness had been attempted in rock music — we need look no further than Little Richard in the 1950's and David Bowie in the 70's for examples. But there had never previously been quite so much experimentation with appearance as was going on in the early 80's. For moat it was just bizarre minor of changes to the hair and makeup, which reflected more of an attempt to be different than conveying any sexual overtones. For others, it meant whole-heatedly adopting ideas, clothes and mannerisms which actively questioned male / female genders. It worked for some, like Boy George of Culture Club and Marilyn of Dead or Alive, as well as Grace Jones in the opposite direction. It also worked for Annie Lennox of Eurythmics — which proved to be a blessing, but also a cross to be borne. On the positive side, the problems lasted for only a short time.

Born December 25, 1954 in Aberdeen, Scotland, Lennox had become quite skilled at the piano and flute by the time she was ready for university and had been awarded a scholarship to the Royal Academy of Music in London. Not finding school to her liking, she eventually dropped out and began working in the London area at a variety of jobs while trying to perform music at night. In making the switch from student to struggling artist, Lennox had met up with a songwriter / guitarist by the name of Dave Stewart and the two hit it off both professionally and personally.

Lennox and Stewart began working on music together, and with guitarist Peter Coombes formed a band called Catch in 1977. They recorded just one single before reforming as

The Tourists in late 1978. The Tourists were caught in up the wavering punk movement and the emerging new wave and romantic genres that were creeping into the Britian in the late 1970's. These influences were quite evident in the band's music. They did well and had three albums on the UK charts before they broke up in 1980.

Accompanying the Tourist's disbanding was the dismantling of Stewart's and Lennox's romantic relationship. For some, such a breakup would be the end of a working relationship as well, but that wasn't the case with these two as they began working on demos for a new band called Eurythmics. The new band signed with RCA and released its first album, IN THE GARDEN, in 1981.

The album did well in the UK, but was almost unheard of in the US. Instead, it was their second album that broke them worldwide (and especially in the States), SWEET DREAMS (ARE MADE OF THIS). It was then that most of the public got its first glimpse of Lennox in all her androgynous glory, and it was quite startling (at least to American sensibilities). Watching that early music video for the album's title track (which enjoyed a lot of MTV airplay), you could hardly take your eyes off Annie Lennox. Shocking, cropped red hair; a well tailored men's suit; and a devious smile — all of these features revealed a woman quite unlike both the happy pop singers of the past and the self-hating punk singers of the late 1970's. With strong sexual overtones of both the song and the video, Lennox came off as not just a singer, but also a menacing sexual force, questioning the standard role models. And all within a four-minute song.

It was an image that stuck, especially after the release of the second single, *Who's That Girl?*, which featured Lennox as both the male and female lovers in the video. With the further sexual obsessions of the lyrics and video for *Love Is A Stranger* (from the first album, but reissued to renewed interest thanks to SWEET DREAMS), Eurythmics were becoming known as a gender-bender band.

That, however, wasn't so much Eurythmics goal as it was a reflection of the times. In fact, their next album, TOUCH, while devling into dark lyricals and electronic-based music, also had some very upbeat musical moments. But the videos were what set the tone, and Eurythmics had become known as a dance-oriented group with dark lyrical inclinations. And while the androgynous look had quickly become their stereotype, by the time of the third and fourth singles from the album, it was quite evident that Stewart and Lennox were moving away from the on-the-edge look of the earlier videos.

Quite aside from the public's perceptions, Stewart and Lennox were serious musicians and became involved in the soundtrack album for a British film production of the George Orwell novel, 1984. Although featuring the same electronic-based arrangements typical of the first two albums, the 1984 soundtrack did poorly on the charts. With concern over the preconceived image with which audiences seemed to be viewing them, Eurythmics decided to move towards a more direct, soul-influenced, Rock and Roll sound with the next album, BE YOURSELF TONIGHT. This album was a much bigger success than 1984, including three Top 30 singles, and Lennox's voice, rather than her appearance, was now the deciding factor — drawing people to the music, especially with the operatically orchestrated *There Must Be an Angel*.

Though they continued to record albums over the next few years, the buying public's interest had shifted into other directions and sales dropping. Lennox and Stewart were starting to drift artistically away from each other as well, and both began exploring other projects. For Annie, the first project outside of Eurythmics was a duet with Al Green, Jackie DeShannon's hit *Put a Little Love in Your Heart* from the soundtrack of the film SCROOGED. It was became a Top 10 hit and showed Annie the definite possibility of success as a solo artist.

Which is exactly what happened. After the hard rocking album WE TOO ARE ONE, Stewart and Lennox decided to take time away from Eurythmics, both working on solo projects. By the end of 1990 it was apparent to all that the band was no more. Lennox had wanted to take some time to have a child, while also working on what would become her first solo album, DIVA. When the album was released in 1992, it became a huge success in both the US and the UK, proving that she had just as much hit potential as a solo artist as she did as part of Eurythmics. She followed it up in 1995 with MEDUSA, which went Platinum.

With all of her success as a solo artist, you might think that Lennox would shy away from anything accosiated with the earlier days of Eurythmics and an image that once almost suffocated them. But that wasn't the case with Lennox or Stewart, and in 1999 they got back together again (as quietly and slyly as they had broken up nearly ten years before) and recorded a new album called POWER. They've toured extensively for the album since then, showing that once people are secure with their abilities, there's always room to go home again.

Selected Studio Albums (as part of Eurythmics):
- ○ IN THE GARDEN (RCA, 1981)
- ○ SWEET DREAMS (ARE MADE OF THIS) (RCA, 1983)
- ○ TOUCH (RCA, 1983)
- ○ 1984 (FOR THE LOVE OF BIG BROTHER) (RCA, 1984)
- ○ BE YOURSELF TONIGHT (RCA, 1985)
- ○ REVENGE (RCA, 1986)
- ○ SAVAGE (RCA, 1987)
- ○ WE TOO ARE ONE (Arista, 1989)
- ○ PEACE (Arista, 1999)

Solo Selected Studio Albums:
  - DIVA (Arista, 1992)
  - MEDUSA (Arista, 1995)

Best of the "Best Of" Albums:
  - GREATEST HITS (Arista, 1991)

Live Albums:
  - LIVE 1983 — 1989 (Arista, 1993)
  - WALKING ON BROKEN GLASS (Arista, 1992)

~ 30 ~
Courtney Love

It could be argued that Courtney Love belongs in a later section of this book, being only one part of the rock group Hole, and therefore not established as an innovative artist on her own. But, just as Debbie Harry was the center of Blondie, Grace Slick of Jefferson Airplane, and Chrissie Hynde of The Pretenders, so too has Love been the center of Hole. After all, without the influences Love has exhibited over the years, both inside the band and out, there would hardly be a Hole to talk about. Additionally, just as the rest of the performers in this book influenced other musicians through their work, so too has Love.

Born Michelle Harrison on July 9, 1965 (some sources state 1964), she was renamed Courtney Michelle Harrison by her mother after splitting from her father. Her mother was a therapist who commuted with Courtney back and forth from New Zealand to Oregon while she was growing up, leaving Courtney in a constant state of flux. Eventually, Courtney left home and move to Portland, Oregon where she first attempted to setup a band on her own.

After a period when she had traveled to many places around the world (using a trust fund set in her name), she returned to Portland and tried out as the lead singer in the band Faith No More. Although she got the job, she left it after only a few shows and worked with future L7 member Jennifer Finch and future Babes In Toyland member Kat Bjelland to form a band called Sugar Babylon. When Courtney was dropped from the band, she decided to travel again, ending up with small roles in two Alex Cox films: SID AND NANCY and STRAIGHT TO HELL.

In 1989 she moved to Los Angeles, determined to start a band on her own. After getting responses to a local newspaper ad, Hole was created. The band persued a fusion of grunge mixed with a heavy dose of punk and released their first EP through Sub Pop, called RAT BASTARD, in 1990. The EP did so well that a second one, DICKNAIL, followed it in March 1991. Both sold well and caught the interest of Caroline Records, who

courtesy Rock Classics

released the band's first full-length album band in 1991, PRETTY ON THE INSIDE.

The album was a critical success, combining the bleak imagery of the grunge movement with a vocal style from Love that bordered on a cross between Wendy O. Williams and Stevie Nicks. Top that off with the fact that the band was made up primarily of women, and the interest factor was high in many quarters — a unique spectacle in the grunge world where the norm was a guy on stage in a plaid shirt and torn jeans strumming a guitar. For many, Hole was the first public showing of the "riot grrrl" image that became a sub-genre of the grunge / alternative movement of the early 1990's.

Love built on that image with a public persona very reminiscent of the punk rhetoric of the mid-70's. Being outspoken, of course, played on that image, and being violently outspoken played added even more to the image. Love seemed to enjoy playing as much as anyone could with that image could.

There's no getting around the publicity that came with Love marrying fellow guitarist Kurt Cobain (of the band Nirvana) in 1992. Although there was (and still is) no reason to suggest that their marriage was done for the publicity, to have two major talents of the punk movement together under one domestic roof was certainly something that fans speculated about at the time. As far as their bands went, however, there seemed to be a strict separation — Kurt continued with Nirvana and Love did the same with Hole.

1994 saw the release of the second full-length album from Hole, LIVE THROUGH THIS, which was getting good press even before its release. Unfortunately, bigger news hit with the suicide of Cobain, which crowded out news of everything else in the rock music world. Interviews and reviews focused on Love and her relationship with Cobain instead of the music on the new album, leaving Love emotionally drained and edgy during the touring that followed the album's release. When bassist Kristen Pfaff overdosed on heroin within weeks of the album's release (a drug that both Cobain and Love had been known for using at one time or another), it lead to even more strain on Love and the band.

Love continued to work with the band and managed to make it through the touring without self-destructing (although she did at times take it out others, sometimes deservedly so). To many, it was a surprise, as the press and some in the public had assumed that they were to witness a type of bizarre "Sid and Nancy" replay, with the roles reversed and Love in the Sid role. Instead, Love came out of the situation stronger than before and ready to try her hand again in acting. When she got good reviews of her work in the film THE PEOPLE VS. LARRY FLINT, a new respect for her emerged in the entertainment industry. Instead of just being considered weird, she had taken on the role of "talented" as well. Of course, the fans who'd stuck by her with Hole knew that already.

With her image changing in the eyes of the public, the image of the band was changing as well. Determined to make an album that would make people respect the band's work, Love and the others worked with Billy Corgan of Smashing Pumpkins on the next album, taking a long time to put it together. The album, CELEBRITY SKIN, was finally released in 1998 and once again received much critical praise, both for the lyrics and for the advancement musically, from the early punk sounds of the first album to the smoothness of the new one.

To some fans, however, it seemed as if Hole was now a bit too smooth, and their focus a bit too polished. Love, meanwhile, was stating in interviews that she saw the album as the one that would really impress people — the one that would be compared to the great rock albums of other artists. It was the image that she was looking for when the album was being put together.

Love, in fact, seemed to be putting more emphasis on the listeners' reactions than the music itself, so that, although she'd always tried to display a disregard for image, it was obvious that the reaction to the new album was more important than the album itself. Which may be why some fans were left undecided about Hole after the album's release. Here was an artist who had always taken a position of not caring what people thought of the music or of her personally, and it was an attitude that fit in well with the grunge / alternative music attitude. Yet, that wasn't what she was displaying at the time of CELEBRITY SKIN's release. Now all that mattered was people's reactions.

Which was the irony. At a point where Love didn't have to worry anymore about her image, it seemed to be what now moved her.

Studio Albums (as part of Hole):
   ◦ PRETTY ON THE INSIDE (Caroline, 1991)
   ◦ LIVE THROUGH THIS (DGC, 1994)
   ◦ MY BODY, THE HAND GRENADE (EFA, 1997)
   ◦ CELEBRITY SKIN (Geffen, 1998)

~ 31 ~
Darlene Love

The girl groups of the 1960's definitely have their own place in the history of women rockers (and even have their own section in this book). Many of them were singing groups that lasted only for a short time before their record companies found fresh faces or until the singers themselves decided to move on. Many of the girl groups are still remembered today, and some of their singers — such as Diana Ross, Ronnie Spector and Martha Reeves — became well-known outside of their groups. Darlene Love, one of the singers for The Blossoms, is well remembered, although you wouldn't instantly recognize her name if you went only by the credits as given on some of the songs she sang.

Born Darlene Wright in Los Angeles, California on July 26, 1938, Darlene had already become known as a member of the singing group The Blossoms by 1957. She was also well-known as a studio vocalist by the time that Phil Spector caught up with The Blossoms in the early 1960's. Wanting to release a single for the girl group, The Crystals, Spector used Darlene to record a song that he'd prepared. It turned out to be the biggest hit of The Crystals' career — *He's a Rebel* — which became not only a classic girl group song, but a classic Rock and Roll song.

Banking on Love, Spector also used her and the rest of The Blossoms to record The Crystals' next single, *He's Sure The Boy I Love*. After that, the original Crystals came back to record for Spector and he moved The Blossoms on to their own recordings. Of these, *Wait Till My Bobby Gets Back Home* was their biggest success. But Darlene herself has contributed to a large number of hit records by other people. If you've ever listened to the music of the 60's, you've heard her voice again and again without knowing it.

Darlene Love moved on to other things as time went by and eventually gained a solid career as an actress. She's recorded a few albums on her own since that time and even worked as Cher's background singer for an early 1990's tour, but nothing since has equaled the success of the song not even credited to her group. A shame, as her piercing vocals on *He's a Rebel* marked a true change in production of rock music during the 1960's.

Selected Studio Albums:
- MASTERS (Phil Spector I, 1981)
- PAINT ANOTHER PICTURE (Columbia, 1990)
- BRINGING IT HOME (Chanachie, 1992)
- UNCONDITIONAL LOVE (Harmony, 1998)
- AGE OF MIRACLES (Love Songs, 1999)

Best of the "Best Of" Albums:
- THE BEST OF DARLENE LOVE (ABKCO, 1992)

Live Albums:
- DARLENE LOVE LIVE (Rhino, 1998)

~ 32 ~
Madonna

Born Madonna Louise Veronica Ciccone on August 16, 1958 in Rochester, Michigan, Madonna broke into the music world in 1982 with the release of her dance music track *Everybody*. Before that, Madonna had tried a variety of ways to break into the entertainment business, including forming bands and even appearing in a low budget movie in 1980. The dance music then taking off in the US was the genre in which Madonna her first big break and she continued with it the following year on her first album, titled simply MADONNA.

With the exposure from the music videos done for the album, and the fact that dance music was once again becoming popular (after the fiery demise of disco just a few short years earlier), the album did incredibly well on the chart, eventually selling four million copies in the US alone. For a time it looked as though Madonna had found her place in the center of the dance movement and would stay there, but that all changed with her next album in 1984.

Beginning with the second album, LIKE A VIRGIN, we began to see the promotional side of Madonna breaking out. Looking like a high school cheerleader who was trying to dress like a punk rocker (of course, she was a high school cheerleader and she was trying to dress like a punk rocker), Madonna and the album both were instantly controversial on the strength of the word "virgin" in the title of both the album and the title track single.

The public ate it up and the album hit No. 1. Madonna next went for a Marilyn Monroe look in her video for *Material Girl*, soaking up the glamour of the movie legend into her own persona. She also spent part of 1985 appearing in the movie DESPERATELY SEEKING SUSAN, which was one of the biggest movie hits of her career.

With her new popularity, Madonna's first album was reissued in 1986, as well as a brand new studio album being released in July of the same year. The new album, TRUE BLUE, lived up to expectations of controversy with her teen pregnancy (or, as some believed it to be, anti-abortion) song *Papa Don't Preach*. She followed it with a video for *Open Your Heart* that featured her as a stripper in a peep show, again creating controversy.

1987 brought the release of WHO'S THAT GIRL, an album in support of a movie by the same name that she appeared in that year. The movie flopped, but the album reached No. 7 on the US charts. It was followed by another reissue, this time dance remixes of earlier tracks called YOU CAN DANCE, and then a Christmas album called A VERY SPECIAL CHRISTMAS at the end of the year. She spent most of 1988 on her VIRGIN Tour, but came back in 1988 with another new album, LIKE A PRAYER.

This album faced new controversy even before it was released. Having signed a deal with Pepsi Cola to appear in a commerical for their product, Madonna put together a commercial which featured excerpts from her upcoming video for the title track of her new album. The video, featuring Madonna at one point singing in front of a row of burning crosses, hardly seemed the appropriate thing to for selling soft drinks and was pulled from television within the month.

1990 was a banner year for Madonna. She completed a world tour (BLONDE AMBITIONS), a documentary of the tour (TRUTH OR DARE), another movie role (in DICK TRACY), another studio album (I'M BREATHLESS) and a "best of" collection (THE IMMACULATE COLLECTION). She renegotiated her contract with Warner Brothers in 1992, at the height of her popularity, for a large amount.

1992 saw the release of another film featuring Madonna (in a small role this time), A LEAGUE OF THEIR OWN, which was a big success. She gained additional exposure through the release of her SEX book, which featured a variety of sexually suggestive posed photos of Madonna and others. The book was released just in time for her next album, EROTICA, which reached No. 3 and sold over two million copies in three months. She followed with another album, BEDTIME STORIES, in 1994, but her momentum was starting to slip — critics and some fans saw the album as being simply more of the same, with no progression from EROTICA.

She began repairing her image, wanting to appear more down-to-earth, with the release of the movie EVITA and her next album RAY OF LIGHT in 1998. The movie was another in a series of flops for Madonna, although the studio album convinced fans to give her another chance.

Looking back on her career, it's undeniable that Madonna has exploited herself beyond the limits of what most other

courtesy Rock Classics

performers would have deemed possible. In fact, while there may be those who don't care for her music or her personality, there are few that wouldn't envy Madonna's ability to promote herself effectively.

Selected Studio Albums:
- MADONNA (Sire, 1983)
- LIKE A VIRGIN (Sire, 1984)
- TRUE BLUE (Sire, 1986)
- WHO'S THAT GIRL (Sire, 1987)
- LIKE A PRAYER (Sire, 1989)
- I'M BREATHLESS (Sire, 1990)
- EROTICA (Maverick, 1992)
- BEDTIME STORIES (Maverick, 1994)
- RAY OF LIGHT (Warner Brothers, 1998)

Best of the "Best Of" Albums:
- THE IMMACULATE COLLECTION (Sire, 1990)

Live Albums:
- GIRLIE SHOW (Alex, 1995)

~ 33 ~
Aimee Mann

Music is a business — a creative business, but a business none-the-less. And many times the business overshadows the creative side. That being so, talented people, who have a lot of musical creativity, all too often end up losing out.

Which is pretty much what happened to Aimee Mann. Born August 9, 1960, Aimee went through the typical routine of learning to play and then getting into bands during her early years. By the late 1970's she'd begun playing punk music and was involved in an early formation of the band Ministry for a short while before putting together the band that was to gain her success — 'Til Tuesday. 'Til Tuesday, made up of Mann on bass, Michael Hausman on drums, Joey Pesce on keyboards and Robert Holmes on guitar, started up in 1983 and gained some prominence in the Boston area, at which time they were picked up by Epic records. 1985 saw the release of their album VOICES CARRY, and its title track was their first single. The song was a smash not only on the pop charts but also on the growing MTV cable network.

After the album's release, with the video's focus on Mann, the band began to splinter. When their follow-up album, WELCOME HOME, made only a mediocre showing on the charts, 'Til Tuesday was branded as a one hit wonder, simply living off the visual success of their first single. Further stress was caused by Mann's publicly known romantic problems (first her breaking up with Hausman, then a relationship with songwriter Jules Shear that quickly went sour for being much too public), which left her unable to write for a time.

In 1988, however, the band returned with a good solid studio album called EVERYTHING'S DIFFERENT NOW. But by that time they were already firmly in the category of "so where are they now" and Epic did little to promote the album. Realizing that they could look forward to little support from their label, the band broke up and Mann decided to pursue a solo career.

Which would have been fine if the record business worked on the principle that sometimes bands break up and everyone should be allowed to go his or her own way. Unfortunately, Epic didn't agree to let Mann out of her contract and she spent the next five years negotiating with them before she was able to record on her own. In 1993 she was finally able to sign to Imago and release her first solo album, WHATEVER. The album wasn't a major success, but it did modestly well for a first solo album and received quite a bit of critical acclaim because of the mature level of Mann's songwriting, and her stylish progressive rock sound with just an edge of intensity behind the melody. The Imago label was quite agreeable to a follow-up.

The only problem was that Imago had its own problems. Forced into bankruptcy in 1995, they refused to release Mann from her contract to sign with another label. So she had to wait until late 1995 / early 1996 before her second solo album, I'M WITH STUPID, could be released through Geffen. Thanks to all of the legal entanglements, I'M WITH STUPID followed the same pattern as WHATEVER — excellent reviews and lackluster sales due to poor promotions.

So, thanks to the business side of the record industry, Aimee Mann's creative power as a songwriter and a performer was stifled for an outrageously long time. Her musical style showed signs, even in the mid-1980's, of the form that would become the backbone of more recent artists (Jewell, Alanis Morisette and Sheryl Crow among others), not to mention the more focused look at relationships, from a feminist point of view, that's popular with many of the top female artists today. All in all, it clearly shows that, sometimes, the record industry exhibits just as much understanding of the creative side of music as your average microwave oven.

Fortunately, interest in Mann's music continues to grow. Much of her music appeared in the recent theatrical film, MAGNOLIA, and she released another album in May 2000. Not only should we wish for more material from Aimee in the future, but also that someone in the music "business" recognizes both talent and opportunity and gets behind Aimee Mann the next time around.

Studio Albums (as part of 'Til Tuesday):
- VOICES CARRY (Epic, 1985)
- WELCOME HOME (Epic, 1986)
- EVERYTHING'S DIFFERENT NOW (Epic, 1988)

Solo Selected Studio Albums:
- WHATEVER (Imago, 1993)
- I'M WITH STUPID (Geffen, 1995)
- BACHELOR NO. 2 (Geffen, 2000)
- MAGNOLIA (soundtrack album) (1999)

~ 34 ~
Sarah Mclachlan

A strong songwriter and singer who's made a number of moderately successful albums, Sarah McLachlan will most probably be remembered for being an organizer of the series of concerts called the Lilith Fair.

Born in Halifax, Nova Scotia on January 28, 1968, Sarah started playing guitar and singing when she was still in her teen, even fronting a new wave band called October Game. Soon after leaving that group she started singing more folk-oriented music while pursuing art at the Nova Scotia School of Design. It was this style of music that interested Nettwerk Records and, after some reluctance on Sarah's part over not completing her schooling, she signed with Nettwerk in 1988.

Her first album, TOUCH, was picked up by Arista for international distribution in 1989. Her lyrics fell into a style reminiscent of Tori Amos and Ani Difranco, while her vocals and lyrical orchestrations sounded strangely similar to Celine Dion that time. The album proved to be a strong beginning for Sarah in the alternative rock market. She followed it in 1991 with the album SOLACE, which only continued to build her fan base, both in Canada and the US.

While continuing to grow as a musician with each new album, Sarah's biggest contribution to the field of women rockers was in the organizing a series of concerts featuring women performers. These concerts, given the name Lilith Fair, began in 1996 and featured a large number of women performers (some well-known and some not quite so well-known) from all musical genres.

Lilith Fair continued until 1999, when it was decided to end the series before it became too commercial and lost its intimate flavor, much like Woodstock and Lollapalooza. Since then McLachlan has concentrated on her music, and there are still talks of doing a foreign version of the festival sometime in the near future.

Selected Studio Albums:
  ◦ TOUCH (Arista, 1989)
  ◦ SOLACE (Arista, 1991)
  ◦ FUMBLING TOWARDS ECTASY (Arista, 1994)
  ◦ THE FREEDOM SESSIONS (Nettwerk, 1995)

- RARITIES, B-SIDES AND OTHER STUFF (Nettwerk, 1996)
- SURFACING (Arista, 1997)

Live Albums:
- MIRRORBALL (Arista, 1999)

~ 35 ~
Joni Mitchell

The 1960's were a time for innovation in popular music, not only with the emergence of rock music as a major force, but also in the type of performers that began to dominate the market. In the years before, there were certainly songwriters who were famous, but usually strictly as songwriters. One the othre side of the coin were musicians who were known for their choices of material, typically from a selection of songwriters. Of course, there were a few examples of musician / songwriters who were recognized for performing their own compositions (typically orchestra leaders it seemed), but it in the 1960's things changed and audiences began to expect artists to be able to both write their own music and perform it.

The era of the singer / songwriter really took hold in the 1960's, particularly after artists like Bob Dylan and the Beatles showed that musicians could write excellent songs without outside help. And it worked both ways — there were songwriters who became popular performers in 1960's. Yet, for many, the well ran dry as the 1970's progressed, with even Dylan struggling to get a handle on how to progress. All too many fell into a routine (either through the constraints of the records labels or their own perceptions of personal limits) and in doing so burnt themselves out, doing the same old stuff year after year and not progressing either creatively or in terms of popularity. Most simply adjusted themselves to a smaller market and continued on, writing and playing the material that they felt comfortable with.

Joni Mitchell, on the other hand, never fell into a fixed mode to begin with, so there wasn't any need to break out of one as time went on. Not that she hasn't had to face the prospect of fans and industry representatives trying to put her on a pedestal and then leave her there.

Born Roberta Joan Anderson in Saskatchewan, Canada on November 7, 1943, Joni first became interested in music when she was nine. Stuck in a hospital because of polio, she began singing for other patients to pass the time. As a result of this, she became interested in playing a musical instrument and first picked up the ukulele. She later became a model while attending the Alberta College of Art for a degree in commercial art, but found herself enjoying music more. After performing at a folk festival in 1964, she decided to give music a try as her career.

Although her first performances were basically folk music, she quickly moved away from folk as her guitar playing took on a more blues-like feel and and her music evolved into more of a rock style than the generic folk sound that was popular in the 1960's. Because of this, her musical style continued to change and she began expressing herself more as a songwriter. By 1967, she had become locally known in Detroit, Michigan as a distinctive vocalist and songwriter, which led her to the New York City area and a record deal with Reprise. Her songs were also beginning to get picked by other artists, including Fairport Convention, Tom Rush and Judy Collins, with Collins' rendition of *Both Sides Now* doing very well on the charts.

It was in this atmosphere that she recorded her first album, JONI MITCHELL. It was an album filled with songs written by a lyricist who wanted to tell stories in a poetic fashion instead of the typical love songs and political songs expected from someone from the "folk club" circuit. The label had no idea how to promote the album and left it hanging, leaving to make little more than a ripple on the charts.

Her second album, CLOUDS, was released in 1969 and did better, thanks to a variety of personal appearances, both live and on television. Meanwhile, Mitchell had penned the song that would end up being remembered as the "theme song" for the Woodstock festival, *Woodstock*, which became a major hit for Crosby, Stills, Nash & Young. LADIES OF THE CANYON, which featured one of her most popular hits, *Big Yellow Taxi*, followed in 1970.

By 1971, Joni had gained a following, although it was never quite as large as some of the other artists in the market. Nevertheless, she was well respected by many artists for her songwriting capabilities and Reprise was certain that mild success would be hers as long as she continued in the pop mold that she seemed to have settled into.

From the following album, BLUE in 1971, it was obvious that Joni Mitchell wasn't content to stay in one mode, however. Instead, her music slowly began to encompass a modest jazz feel, coupled with stronger lyrics that dealt with relationships and personal struggles. The label felt some hesitance over the new album, but Joni's popularity continued to swing upward so they left her to her own devices after some initial struggles. Through the album's critical appraisals, Joni found herself being analyzed, by way of her lyrics, in attempts to discover some great history of her life through her singing stories.

Perhaps it could have been considered a sign of great interest on the part of the critics, wanting to invest that much time into her songs, but for Joni it just seemed another example of people assuming that a woman writing songs had to be taking events from her own life — not creative enough to simply "create" the stories.

Joni continued to explore jazz techniques in her songwriting, opening up her musical style to different interpretations instead of going for the folk-pop song that many expected from her. For a time, it continued to hold the attention of the critics and the fans alike, but eventually Joni ventured perhaps a bit too far in that direction with her 1975 album, THE HISSING OF SUMMER LAWNS and 1977's DON JUAN'S RECKLESS DAUGHTER.

Although her popularity has slowly dwindled since the late 1970's, her dedication to making new music hasn't gone away. Her lyric writing has also been consistent and is often cited by other songwriters when discussing abstract poetic intentions and innovations. For every songwriter, be it Kate Bush, Ani DiFranco or Tori Amos, there was an earlier creator of poetic text, a songwriter who laid the groundwork and framed the rules. For many, the source of it all has been Joni Mitchell's albums. Meanwhile, her shift into other musical styles has seen Joni move from acoustic guitar to rock to electronic and then back to acoustic again over the years. In doing so, she's perhaps left a lot of confused label people and reviewers in the dust, while she continues to glide along on her own experiments, redefining her own creative ambitions, and performing music that she enjoys.

Selected Studio Albums:
- JONI MITCHELL (Reprise, 1968)
- CLOUDS (Reprise, 1969)
- LADIES OF THE CANYON (Reprise, 1970)
- BLUE (Reprise, 1971)
- FOR THE ROSES (Asylum, 1972)
- COURT & SPARK (Asylum, 1974)
- THE HISSING OF SUMMER LAWNS (Asylum, 1975)
- HEJIRA (Asylum, 1976)
- DON JUAN'S RECKLESS DAUGHTER (Asylum, 1977)
- MINGUS (Asylum, 1979)
- WILD THINGS RUN FAST (Geffen, 1982)
- DOG EAT DOG (Geffen, 1985)
- CHALK MARK IN A RAIN STORM (Geffen, 1988)
- NIGHT RIDE HOME (Geffen, 1991)
- TURBULENT INDIGO (Reprise, 1994)
- TAMING THE TIGER (Reprise, 1998)
- BOTH SIDES NOW (Reprise, 2000)

Best of the "Best Of" Albums:
- HITS (Reprise, 1996)
- MISSES (Reprise, 1996)

Live Albums:
  ○ MILES OF AISLES (Asylum, 1974)
  ○ SHADOWS & LIGHT (Asylum, 1980)

~ 36 ~
Stevie Nicks

August 24, 1996. It was an all-day concert in Columbus, Ohio with Stevie Nicks and Cher as the headliners. When Cher cancelled at the last minute, it left some audience members disappointed, but not those who'd come to see Stevie. To them it was a rare chance to see her that year on tour.

Stevie's set was going over well with the crowd at the outdoor arena called Polaris Amphitheater. Being a multi-act show, there was no special setup for the stage during Stevie's act — just the band and the microphones, including a center mike with a few scarves tied to it. Eventually, at a latter point in the show, Stevie reached out to grab a scarf, only to find that it was secured quite tightly to the microphone stand. A look of frustration crossed her face as she yanked on the scarf once again.

It was an awkward moment to watch, and certainly frustrating for Stevie. The mood on stage had been broken. A spell had been broken. And if there was one thing Stevie knew about, it was casting magic spells on stage.

courtesy Hot Wacks

Born May 26, 1949, Stevie grew up with her family in a whirlwind of activity thanks to her father, Jess Seth Nicks, working his way up the corporate ladder. He eventually emerged as the president of Armour Foods, General Brewing and executive vice-president of Greyhound, and did with a determination to follow his goals no matter where they sent him, even if that meant transplanting his family to another part of the country. From this came not only Stevie's ability to create on her own, but also a determination of her own to get what she wanted and to stay firm to her ideas of success.

At the age of four, Stevie began being coached by her grandfather, Aaron Jess Nicks, to sing country songs. With this, the two would go to bars and sing to the crowds. It was a short career for Stevie, a career that ended once her parents found out where her grandfather had been taking her, but it opened up a musical world to her that she never let go of. By the time she was in high school, she was already forming groups, including an early one called Changing Times.

Having started in college in the Bay Area, Stevie decided to stay behind when her family moved once again to Chicago in 1968. At San Jose State, where she studied for a degree in speech communication, she met up with Lindsey Buckingham and the two formed a group with Javier Pacheco and Calvin Roper called Fritz. They managed to stay together for a few years and performed as an opening act for many other bands in the area, including Jimi Hendrix, Janis Joplin, Moby Grape and Creedence Clearwater Revival.

It was a good band, but as in the majority of cases, they could only last so long before the members wanted to move on to other projects. After three and a half years, Fritz broke up and Stevie and Lindsey began working together as a duo, while getting by their day jobs.

Like the scarf on the stage twenty-odd years later, the spell had been broken. Everything had come down and hit hard. But it wasn't enough to simply give in, and continuing on as a duo was the next step forward. In 1973, the pair was able to swing a deal with Polydor for an album called BUCKINGHAM NICKS. Although the album did gain them some success — including a following in Birmingham, Alabama of all places — their popularity was not enough to convince Polydor to go ahead with another album.

They went to many other labels with their demo tapes, but there was little interest in the duo. Instead, by 1974, they were working day jobs once again, with Stevie as a waitress in a Beverly Hills restaurant.

Even with another yank, the scarf refused to move. Instead, action came from another and completely unpredictable direction.

In late 1974, Mick Fleetwood had just watched another member of Fleetwood Mac leave. Bob Welch went on to success on his own in the late 1970's, but it left Fleetwood Mac once again with not enough members to carry on. While looking for a replacement, Mick had run into Keith Olsen, an engineer who had his own studio. He had worked on the BUCKINGHAM NICKS album and was eager to get Mick into his studio to record the next Mac album. To demonstrate the studio's output, Olsen played the BUCKINGHAM NICKS demos.

Mick liked what he heard and asked the two to join Fleetwood Mac in time for the next album release in early 1975. The album, which just had the band's name on the cover and no other title, quickly became a Gold album thanks to Christine McVie's single *Over My Head* and then the success of Stevie's *Rhiannon*.

Fleetwood Mac toured for the album and in 1976 went back into the studio to record one of the most successful rock albums of all time — RUMOURS. This album swept the nation and continued on the charts for years before finally falling off, spanning several hits including Stevie's *Gold Dust Woman*. After that, Fleetwood Mac were on top, playing everywhere and becoming one of the top bands in the world.

With success came the innevitable backlash against the group, with Stevie being at the center of most negative comments. Because her lyrics were more poetic in nature, and because several dealt with themes that could be envisioned to be otherworldly, it was easy for critics to let loose at her. Jeers came also from long-time fans of the Mac who saw their original blues generated music being replaced with the rock and pop stylings of Stevie, Lindsey and Christine McVie. Although each had contributed music that was hard edged to the band, the biggest hits were coming from those members who weren't even in the band when it was created. And that bothered some people.

So, Stevie became the scapegoat for those who didn't like Fleetwood Mac. Her performance on stage probably just egged these critics on further. While there were female rockers performing in bands, it wasn't very common to see one with two women in it who shared equal roles (and wrote some of the biggest hits during this period as well). Now here was Christine and Stevie in the forefront of this "blues-oriented" rock band. More so, Stevie's on-stage persona was one that played off of the mysticism in her lyrics — the long dresses, the scarves, the wraps. Even her movements had a strange ballet-like fantasy quality that perhaps suggested to some that she wasn't of this world. No doubt, there were some who thought she wasn't all in this world either.

After the bloated Fleetwood Mac effort of 1979, TUSK — an album that nevertheless was successful and did spring Stevie's *Sara* as a single — and a live album which came out in 1980, Stevie and the others decided to work on projects outside of the band. Stevie's first solo album became a blockbuster hit in 1981 and was called BELLA DONNA.

The album featured several hits for Stevie, including two duets, one with Tom Petty, *Stop Dragging My Heart Around* and one with Don Henley called *Leather and Lace*. More importantly, it featured a song that became one of the biggest hits in Stevie's solo career and turned a few critics' heads, *Edge of Seventeen*. It reached No. 1 and Stevie became known as a solo artist for the first time.

The outside projects of other Mac members went over well, but not to the extent of BELLA DONNA. And this, perhaps, made the first cracks in the foundation of the latest incarnation of Fleetwood Mac.

Stevie tugged again on the scarf to break it free. With no success, she let it go and turned her back on it, looking to the band to start the next song.

Fleetwood Mac got back together in 1982 to record MIRAGE, which was another success for the band, but there was a growing distance between Stevie and the others because of her promotional work and touring for BELLA DONNA. There was also a feeling of too many creative people in band, a common problem after one or more band members going solo for a while. It was a draining experience for everyone involved and lead to a split that lasted close to five years before the release of TANGO IN THE NIGHT in 1987.

In between, Stevie did two more successful albums, THE WILD HEART in 1983, which included the hit *Stand Back*" and the 1985 album ROCK A LITTLE. Stevie's music continued to be a hit making phenomenon and her career as a solo artist gained strength. Yet, the conscious mannerisms of the critics (and some fans) — harping on the "magic" of Stevie's lyrics and the "witch" persona — began to grow wearisome to the reat of the fans and to Stevie herself, as evidenced by some of the interviews at the time. Although willing to admit that her songwriting dealt with fantasy elements, it became clearer in the passing years since *Rhiannon* that, yes, fantasy was an interest of hers, but not her whole life. In fact, real life was taking such a hold on Stevie that she might have wished that the fantasies were more real.

Going back and forth between the band and her solo career began to take its toll. After completing her next solo album, THE OTHER SIDE OF THE MIRROR, in 1989 and then doing the Mac album BEHIND THE MASK, Stevie began to wonder if she needed to give up one for the other. Finally, three years after Lindsey left the band, Stevie left Fleetwood Mac in 1993 and begin work on her next solo album, STREET ANGEL.

It was another great album from Stevie, but the hits were not as forthcoming as they'd been in the past.   More importantly, problems with her health — thanks to a prescribed drug that caused physical and emotional problems — began effecting her performance and the critics, who had for so long wanted something to bring the magic crashing to the ground, used her health problems as a way to get to her.   By the end of the STREET ANGEL tour, Stevie was ready to just stop performing live since the abuse was becoming too great to deal with. Her record contract was also at an end and there was a general feeling of just wanting to stop.

courtesy KAOS2000

She turned back to the scarf and tugged at it. It refused to budge. With both hands, Stevie began pulling on the scarf and the microphone stand starts to wobble under the strain. If fans in the crowd had looked closely, they could have seen a smile slowly coming across Stevie's face.

Although depression would have been the common reaction to these events for most, Stevie's insistence on not letting anything hold her back came came to the fore. Working on her own (with some assistance), she put the decline behind her, lost weight and began working on new material once again. Then, another positive event transpired.

With the revival *Don't Stop* as a Presidential campaign theme song for President Clinton in 1996 came the chance of Fleetwood Mac reuniting once again. With it came success that lead not only to a tour, but also the 1997 album THE DANCE, featuring the same band members who had given the world their "white album" through TANGO IN THE NIGHT. Also a three-CD boxed-set of Stevie's work came out in 1998, THE ENCHANTED WORKS OF STEVIE NICKS and quickly went Gold.

In 1999 production began on a new Stevie Nicks album, with Sheryl Crow as producer. Meanwhile, other artists have been re-examining the fantasy and mystical visions aspects of Stevie's work over the years — many readily admitting that Stevie's work was a major influence on their own writing. So, while it looked for a time as if the story wouldn't have a happy ending, there's no need to worry. The world goes on and it's apparent that Stevie knows that there'll also be another time, another song.

Stevie swung the scarf back in forth, watched the stand swaying, and bent over, as if pulling with all her might to make the scarf come loose. She then stood up and tried to untie it, but it was tied too tightly. Finally, with a smile, she lets go of the scarf and watches it flutter back down to the side of the stand. The magic was broken with the irony of reality, but it mattered little. It was replaced with the magic of whimsy. The magic of the real world. The magic of life.

Solo Selected Studio Albums:
- BELLA DONNA (Modern, 1981)
- THE WILD HEART (Modern, 1983)
- ROCK A LITTLE (Modern, 1985)
- THE OTHER SIDE OF THE MIRROR (Modern, 1989)
- STREET ANGEL (Modern, 1994)

Best of the "Best Of" Albums:
- TIMESPACE — THE BEST OF STEVIE NICKS (Modern, 1991)
- THE ENCHANTED WORKS OF STEVIE NICKS (Modern, 1998)

Selected Studio Albums (as part of Buckingham Nicks):
- BUCKINGHAM NICKS (Polydor, 1973)

Selected Studio Albums (as part of Fleetwood Mac):
- FLEETWOOD MAC (Reprise, 1975)
- RUMOURS (Reprise, 1977)
- TUSK (Reprise, 1979)
- MIRAGE (Reprise, 1982)
- TANGO IN THE NIGHT (Reprise, 1987)

○ BEHIND THE MASK (Reprise, 1990)
○ THE DANCE (Reprise, 1997)

Live Albums (as part of Fleetwood Mac):
○ FLEETWOOD MAC LIVE (Reprise, 1980)

Best of the "Best Of" Albums (as part of Fleetwood Mac):
○ FLEETWOOD MAC'S GREATEST HITS (Reprise, 1988)
○ THE CHAIN (Reprise, 1992)

~ 37 ~
Laura Nyro

Sometimes an artist will create a body of work that is innovative, groundbreaking and creative, and yet it doen't meet with the success and popularity it deserves. Some watch their material become truly popular only after other artists have interpretted it in their own ways. The music may be successful, but it's not the same sense of accomplishment for the original artist, who doesn't enjoy success first hand.

Such was the case for Laura Nyro. Born Laura Nigro on October 18, 1947 in New York City, Laura was the daughter of a jazz musician, so she naturally became interested in music at an early age. She wrote her first song at the age of eight and attended the High School of Music and Art in Manhattan. She'd also begun playing piano and some guitar in clubs around the New York area, her material mostly jazz and rock. Her first album was released in 1966 with a title that not many would have braved, MORE THAN A NEW DISCOVERY, but it did poorly in sales. The songs on the album were considered excellent, however, and many of the tracks were later hits for other artists (including *Wedding Bell Blues* and *Blowin' Away* for the Fifth Dimension, *Stoney End* for Barbra Streisand and *And When I Die* for Blood, Sweat and Tears). It was a definite sign of what Nyro was to come to expect.

She next appeared at the Monterey Pop Festival, which would become known as the explosive debut for both Janis Joplin and Jimi Hendrix, but that wasn't the case for Nyro. Booed off the stage for a set that was introverted and delicate — where most of the other artists were bombastic and showy — Nyro was somewhat unnerved. On the bright side, however, was that the peformance led her meeting up with David Geffen, who at the time was working for a music agency, and Geffen enjoyed the set so much that he offered to become Nyro's manager. This led to her obtaining a contract with Columbia and recording her 1968 album, ELI AND THE THIRTEENTH CONFESSION. This album, a concept album based on the life of a girl growing up, was met with good critical response, but buyers just weren't interested. Instead, Nyro once again saw songs being lifted from the album and turned into hits by other artists (including the Fifth Dimension once again with *Stoned Soul Picnic* and *Sweet Blindness* and Three Dog Night with *Eli's Comin'*).

There was frustration from Columbia's standpoint, since several people involved with Nyro felt that many of her songs could become major hits for her if she'd just open up a bit and develop the songs in a hit-making fashion. Laura, however, wasn't interested in writing hits, only in writing material that she wanted to hear herself, and after refusing to budge on the issue, Columbia let her record the albums as she saw fit.

Fortunately, for Nyro, that seemed to work with the release of her next album, NEW YORK TENDABERRY, in 1969. This album had more promotion and two singles did well: *Time and Love* and *Save the Country*. Popularity began to wane again with her 1970 release CHRISTMAS AND THE BEADS OF SWEAT, on which she attempted more soul-oriented music. A follow-up album of cover songs, GONNA TAKE A MIRACLE, didn't fare much better.

Frustrated by the lack of sales and the realization that there was insufficient interest in what she really wanted to do with her music, Nyro left the record business in 1971 to get married. By 1975, however, she was freshly divorced and back into music with a new album called SMILE. She followed up with a live album called SEASON OF LIGHTS in 1977 and another studio album called NESTED in 1978, but there still seemed to be little interest in her music, so she decided to leave the business again in 1978.

From there, Nyro essentially gave up on recording and performing, recording only two more studio albums between 1978 and her death from cancer in 1997. At the time of her death, a tribute album to Laura Nyro was just about to be released which would show listeners in the rock world once again how good Nyro's writing was. Unfortunately, she didn't get to see the resurgence of interest in her music that the tribute would have meant. Instead, Laura Nyro remains a semi-forgotten name. Although many know her songs, far fewer know the artist who created them.

Selected Studio Albums:
- MORE THAN A NEW DISCOVER (Verve, 1967)
- ELI AND THE THIRTEENTH CONFESSION (Columbia, 1968)
- NEW YORK TENDABERRY (Columbia, 1969)
- CHRISTMAS AND THE BEADS OF SWEAT (Columbia, 1970)
- GONNA TAKE A MIRACLE (Columbia, 1971)
- SMILE (Columbia, 1976)
- NESTED (Columbia, 1978)

  ○ MOTHER'S SPIRITUAL (Columbia, 1984)
  ○ WALK THE DOG AND LIGHT THE LIGHT (Columbia, 1993)

Best of the "Best Of" Albums:
  ○ STONED SOUL PICNIC: THE BEST OF LAURA NYRO (Sony, 1997)

Live Albums:
  ○ SEASON OF LIGHTS (Columbia, 1997)
  ○ LIVE AT THE BOTTOM LINE (Cypress, 1990)

~ 38 ~
Suzi Quatro

The US, at times, has been absolutely remarkable for missing some of its own national treasures when it comes to rock music. Especially when it comes to good old, down-to-earth, solid rock music. One has to wonder why people like Jimi Hendrix and The Ramones had to find success overseas first before gaining acclaim at home. How many others have passed us (or rather, US) right by.

Case in point: Suzi Quatro. Born June 3, 1950 in Detroit, Michigan, Suzi was one of five children (three sisters and a brother) in a family that emphasized music. By the time she was eight, Suzi was playing bongos in her father's trio and was already trying to form her own band at school. With her sisters, Patti (who would later join the successful all-women band, Fanny) and Arlene, Suzi had her first professional band, The Pleasure Seekers. They became fairly well-known in the Detroit area and eventually end up touring parts of the country and beyond. They even recorded a couple of singles.

They were a rock band that played good solid Rock and Roll. However, by 1967 the times were changing and playing good old fashion rock music was not considered the "in" thing to be doing. It was the time of SGT. PEPPER and THE ACID TEST. Cutting loose with an old Elvis song didn't do it in many of the "hip" quarters of the day and the members of The Pleasure Seekers knew it. The only way to stay competitive in the US music scene at that time was to follow the trend, and so the band regrouped, added Suzi's 16 year old sister Nancy, and became the hard rock band, The Cradle in 1969.

Which they believed was a step in the right direction. Unfortunately, as time went on, it became obvious that the drive which had kept the band together when they were playing straight forward Rock and Roll was dissipating with their change in musical style. It showed in their performances as well — instead of a resurgence of energy, the band began falling apart. But not straight away, and while they were working hard to make it last, an important event happened that would catapult Suzi to the next level in the rock world.

Arriving in Detroit to produce Jeff Beck at Motown Studios, UK producer Mickie Most was offered the chance to check out The Cradle performing. Taking up the offer, he was left without much in the way of enthusiasm for the band itself, but was struck by the five foot bass player in the background. Feeling that Suzi had a presence that shone during the performance, Most offered Suzi the chance to work with him back in England. Suzi wasn't thrilled with the idea of leaving her sisters behind once Most made it clear that he was only interested in her. Nevertheless, they agreed that if nothing became of The Cradle, Suzi would be in touch.

By 1971, everyone in The Cradle was ready to call it a day and move on to other things. For Suzi this meant contacting Mickie Most in England. Fortunately, Most was still interested and Suzi arrived in London during late 1971. Most, to Suzi's dismay however, was not ready to just turn her loose on the public, and instead had Suzi work on material to record. When her first single *Rolling Stone*, failed to chart and a showcase performance turned sour, Suzi was for a brief moment unsure if it was worth all the trouble of continuing. But these thoughts were fleeting and with the help of two songwriters that Most had taken into his studio named Mick Chapman and Nicky Chinn, Suzi released her next single, *Can the Can*. It became a No. 1 song in the UK, Japan, Australia and parts of Europe as well.

Also in 1973 was the release of Suzi's first album, the self-titled SUZI QUATRO. With the album, she began raking up hit after hit on the UK charts. In the US, even with the Bell label backing the album, there was only minor interest, with *Can the Can* only reaching No. 56 on the US charts (in 1975 when it was finally released), even with Suzi gaining maximum press opening for Alice Cooper on his WELCOME TO MY NIGHTMARE tour.

Why there was no success in the US seems very odd, until we examine the US musical scene at the time, where most bands were either diving into expanded epic "concept albums," or living at the other extreme doing the dance music which was slowly morphing into disco. So, while some bands were still playing the standard two or three guitars rock music, like KISS and the Ramones, they were considered "behind the times" and old fashion. She even tried dressing the part of a greaser, all in black leather and with a street punk's attitude in her songs. It was a style that would be the genesis of The Runaways in the middle 1970's (and the early look of Joan Jett's solo career as well) and be successful for others, but Suzi was just too soon. And although she was one of the original punkers of the early 1970's, she fell into that class of bands that were loved in some quarters, but more generally dispised for not being "with it."

Not that any of this was a major problem for Suzi. The first album had done well and her follow-up albums, QUATRO and YOUR MAMA WON'T LIKE ME, succeeded in Europe and other (non-US) countries as well. Interest in the US finally came when the producers of the hit television series HAPPY DAYS began scouting for an actress / musician to play an on-going character named "Leather" Tuscadero. After they'd seen her on the cover of Rolling Stone, Suzi was asked to join the show and made seven appearances over a year's time.

With the new attention in America, we might have expected a turn for the better in Suzi's US popularity. That wasn't quite the case. Although her next album, IF YOU KNEW SUZI, was the first to break the US Top 40 Albums, and a single from the album, *Stumblin' In* went to No. 4 on the charts, it was the peak of Suzi's success in the US. So she went back to concentrating on recording after her brush with television and 1980 brought the release of her album ROCK HARD. It was an album filled with an almost heavy metal edge, but it was too much, too soon. The whole heavy metal genre was still at least two years off in the US and the album failed to make the Top 40.

By 1982, things had changed somewhat in Suzi's life. She had given birth to her daughter, Laura, and there was talk about returning to television in the UK. After recording the album MAIN ATTRACTION, which failed to make waves on the charts, and recording another album in 1983 (that wasn't released until 1998), Suzi decided to hold off of touring and recording and concentrate on her family and television instead.

That's not the end of the story, though. In 1986 Suzi appeared in a production of ANNIE GET YOUR GUN produced for the London's West End. The late 1980's saw her touring again, which lead directly to another album called OH SUZI Q in 1990. Since that time she's worked on new material, appeared on television in a variety of programs in the UK (she made a brief appearance as herself in an episode of ABSOLUTELY FABULOUS), and even co-wrote a musical based on screen actress Tallulah Bankhead called TALLULAH WHO.

At the turn on the century, Suzi is still performing and working on new material. The first part of the year 2000 saw Suzi going on tour in Australia with her daughter, a musician in her own right, performing with her. Fan interest in Suzi is high as well and another album may come fairly soon to fans who've been listening to her for over 25 years now.

So, the Detroit girl never quite caught on in the States. But, overall, she really hasn't anything to be sorry about, considering her accomplishments over the years.

Solo Selected Studio Albums:
- ○ SUZI QUATRO (Bell/RAK, 1973)
- ○ QUATRO (Bell/RAK, 1974)
- ○ YOUR MAMA WON'T LIKE ME (Arista/RAK, 1975)
- ○ AGGRO PHOBIA (RAK, 1977)
- ○ IF YOU KNEW SUZI (RAK, 1978)
- ○ SUZI . . . AND OTHER FOUR-LETTER WORDS (RSO/RAK, 1979)
- ○ ROCK HARD (Dreamland, 1980)
- ○ MAIN ATTRACTION (Polydor, 1982)
- ○ UNRELEASED EMOTION (Connoisseur, recorded 1983 and released 1998)
- ○ OH SUZI Q (1990)

Best of the "Best Of" Albums:
- ○ ORIGINAL HITS (RAK, 1992)
- ○ THE WILD ONE — CLASSIC QUATRO (Razor & Tie, 1996)
- ○ GREATEST HITS (EMI, 2000)

Live Albums:
- ○ LIVE AND KICKIN' (Alex, 1977)

~ 39 ~
Bonnie Raitt

Sometimes success is slow in coming. And even when a performer is well-known in critical and professional circles, success isn't measured by who you are, but by how many records you can sell. For some, having more talent than many others in the business doesn't equate with popularity. And you can count on the thumbs of one foot the number of times that a record company kept anyone on its roster when the return on their investment didn't cover their costs.

Bonnie Raitt found herself in exactly that situation. She also found, at that same time, that the image she had of herself was of someone on the spiraling road to self-destruction. In both cases, however, Raitt was able to turn those harbingers of hopelessness around and build upon them to finally achieve the success she so deserved.

Born November 8, 1949 in Burbank, California, her father was the famed Broadway star John Raitt (best known for his roles in CAROUSEL and KISS ME KATE). With music already in the family, it's no surprise that Bonnie took it up herself. Growing up with brothers, she turned into a tomboy and, as a result, pursued a more aggressive style in her music than generally forthcoming from female performers. She was hooked on the blues, especially the use of bottleneck slide on the guitar, and after first picking up a guitar at the age of twelve, that was the type of music that she mostly played.

Although she went to college in 1967, she ended up playing full time in folk clubs and coffee houses in the Boston area. Within acouple of years she had gained a cult following and was playing in many of the clubs along the US East Coast, sticking with blues and folk music for the most part.

In 1971 Warner Brothers signed her and her first album was released that same year. The album was a huge critical success, and many fellow musicians were impressed by Raitt's work. That, however, didn't translate into sales and Raitt found herself in the meager position of respected musician — popular with people in the business and recognized as an excellent guitarist — but doing only so-so in sales. Some hope was gained in 1977 with the release of her album SWEET FORGIVENESS (which featured a popular remake of Del Shannon's *Runaway*), but by 1986 Warner Brothers had ended their contract with Raitt following the slow sales of her ninth album, NINE LIVES. It was a depressing development, and it was coupled with the knowledge that she was slowly drinking herself into oblivion as well.

While never into the drug scene, as were many other rock artists of the 1970's, Raitt had found herself increasingly involved with alcohol, thanks to its unfortunate reputation as being prerequisite for a blues artist. At first it was all part of the image, but eventually she realized that it was slowing her down and holding her back. In 1987 she decided to stop drinking, while also considering available options for restarting her record career. In the meantime, Raitt continued with her long-time support of numerous political causes with appearances at festivals around the country and the world.

In 1989 Raitt recorded an album for Capitol, her new label, entitled NICK OF TIME. The album, produced by Don Was, became the record that truly broke Raitt through, on the charts, and into the public eye. Not only did it stay on the charts for two years, but it earned numerous awards at the 1990 Grammy Awards, proving its popularity and success. It was the turning point that set Raitt's career onto a steady course and she's continued releasing a new album every 2 to 3 years since then with success.

So, Bonnie Raitt has proved not only that there's always a chance to turn things around and prove yourself to the world, but that sometimes the best things really do come to those who wait — and believe in themselves while they wait.

Selected Studio Albums:
- BONNIE RAITT (Warner Brothers, 1971)
- GIVE IT UP (Warner Brothers, 1972)
- TAKIN' MY TIME (Warner Brothers, 1973)
- STREETLIGHTS (Warner Brothers, 1974)
- HOMEPLATE (Warner Brothers, 1975)
- SWEET FORGIVENESS (Warner Brothers, 1977)
- THE GLOW (Warner Brothers, 1979)
- GREEN LIGHT (Warner Brothers, 1981)
- NINE LIVES (Warner Brothers, 1986)
- NICK OF TIME (Capitol, 1989)
- LUCK OF THE DRAW (Capitol, 1991)
- LONGING IN THEIR HEARTS (Capitol, 1994)
- ROAD TESTED (Capitol, 1995)
- FUNDAMENTAL (Capitol, 1998)

Best of the "Best Of" Albums:
- THE BONNIE RAITT COLLECTION (Warner Brothers, 1990)

~ 40 ~
Linda Ronstadt

There's no doubt about it, Linda Ronstadt was one of the most popular female rock singers of the 1970's. It seemed for a time that it was impossible to keep her off of the charts, and nearly impossible to turn on the radio without hearing one of her songs in only a matter of minutes. She demonstrated, in an era where the singer / songwriters were the rule of the day, that someone who was simply singer could also be creative, re-interpreting existing songs and making them into new hits. She also showed that a singer didn't have to be locked into a single musical genre to remain successful.

Born July 15, 1946 in Tucson, Arizona, Linda grew up listening to her father singing Mexican songs (from his native country) and the musical outlets of her brother Mike and sister Suzi. By the age of 14 she was singing with her siblings as The Three Ronstadts (also known as The New Union Ramblers), a folk-style singing group.

After going to the University of Arizona for one semester, she dropped out and traveled to Los Angeles with guitarist Bob Kimmel and later joined up with guitarist Kenny Edwards to form a folk band called The Stone Poneys. By 1965 the trio was performing at The Troubadour and was soon picked up by Mercury Records. Following changes in name (to The Signets) and musical style (both suggested by the label) that led nowhere, they reverted back to their original name. The Stone Poneys released three albums, but it's their second, EVERGREEN, VOL. 2, that's best remembered, providing as it did the group's biggest hit, *Different Drum*, written by Michael Nesmith. It was the first time that many people had heard Linda's voice, and her forceful, yet clear voice gave a pleasant lift to the song.

After one more album in 1968, the group broke up and Linda signed as a solo artist with Capitol. Her first album, HAND SOWN HOME GROWN, was released in 1969 and did little on the charts, but her second in 1970, SILK PURSE, produced the Top 40 single with *Long, Long Time*. Both albums showed Linda's folk roots, and also a mild country twang. These early albums provided some of the first signs of the country-rock genre that would emerge as a major phenomenon of the 1970's with the success of bands like Little Feat and The Eagles.

courtesy Hot Wacks

As a side note, several members of The (then future) Eagles first worked together on Linda's third album, LINDA RONSTADT. Although those musicians went on to great success as The Eagles, Linda's album did only so-so on the charts. And then disaster struck. Working on a new album for the Asylum record label, she watched production going out of control, and at the same time, Capitol was demanding another studio album. All of this left Linda in a very difficult financial position. When the Asylum album, titled DON'T CRY NOW, was finally released in 1973 it reached an only moderately respectful No. 45 on the US charts.

But what the album did do was introduce Linda to Peter Asher (formerly of Peter & Gordon), who helped her with production on her final Capitol album, HEART LIKE A WHEEL. Although, this album was done strictly as a contractual obligation, it ended up being the one to cement Linda's success in the 1970's and the style that would carry her for the next several years. As well as extending the country flavor of her music, she also selected older hit songs, reinterpreting them in her own style. With the Top 2 successes of covers for *You're No Good* and *When Will I Be Loved*, Linda was now in a position to do her albums the way she saw fit.

Moving back to Asylum, Linda followed the pattern set by HEART LIKE A WHEEL, both by working with Peter Asher and by reintroducing older hits done in her own style. By 1978, she had begun expanding upon that formula by reinterpreting a series of songs from the emerging new wave era, including material from Elvis Costello. It continued to work for Linda and she continued to have hits, but after the mediocre success of GET CLOSER, Linda decided to take a break from recording and work in another field all together — Broadway and Gilbert & Sullivan.

The Broadway production of PIRATES OF PENZANCE did so well that a movie adaptation was filmed in 1981. Both the movie and the Broadway production showcased Linda's operatic range and led to her returning to the recording studio in another genre altogether, reproducing lush ballads from the 1930's and 40's. WHAT'S NEW was released in 1983 and was followed in 1984 and 86 by two more albums of similar material. In doing this, Ronstadt was continuing with her reinterpretations older standards, and was only moving further back in time to select her songs.

courtesy Hot Wacks

This phase only lasted three years, after which Linda decided to go back to recording more contemporary material, beginning with the theme from the movie AN AMERICAN TAIL, *Somewhere Out There* (a duet with James Ingram) and the country album TRIO with Dolly Parton and Emmylou Harris. After that, however, she embarked upon another side trip into the past by recording an album of Mexican songs that she remembered her father singing to her as a child. The album CANCIONES DE MI PADRE eventually reached Platinum in the US and could be seen as evidence that Spanish language music could have a regular place in the pop charts on a basis (coinciding with the emergence of Gloria Estefan and the Miami Sound Machine at around the same time).

From 1989 onward, Linda has moved around in different musical genres, seemingly with no fixed objectives other than to sing the music she wanted to sing — be it country, Latin-flavored, rock, or anything in between. A boxed-set collection of her material was released in 1999, and there is still talk of another album. But, in consideration of some minor vocal ailments and a desire to spend her time raising her family, Linda has recently considered withdrawing from recording, at least the time being.

If she does record another album, it's a safe bet that, given her past versatility, no-one will be trying to second-guess what the material might be.

Selected Studio Albums (as part of the Stone Poneys):
- STONE PONEYS FEATURING LINDA RONSTADT (Capitol, 1967)
- EVERGREEN, VOL. 2 (Capitol, 1967)
- STONE PONEYS & FRIENDS, VOL. 3 (Capitol, 1968)

Selected Studio Albums:
- HAND DOWN HOME GROWN, 1970)
- LINDA RONSTADT (Capitol, 1971)
- DON'T CRY NOW (Asylum, 1973)
- HEART LIKE A WHEEL (Capitol, 1974)
- PRISONER IN DISGUISE (Asylum, 1975)
- HASTEN DOWN THE WIND (Asylum, 1976)
- SIMPLE DREAMS (Asylum, 1977)
- LIVING IN THE U.S.A. (Asylum, 1978)
- MAD LOVE (Asylum, 1980)
- GET CLOSER (Asylum, 1982)
- WHAT'S NEW (Asylum, 1983)
- LUSH LIFE (Asylum, 1984)
- FOR SENTIMENTAL REASONS (Asylum, 1986)
- CANCIONES DE MI PADRE (Asylum, 1987)
- CRY LIKE A RAINSTORM — HOWL LIKE THE WIND (Asylum, 1989)
- MAS CANCIONES (Asylum, 1990)
- FRENESI (Asylum, 1992)
- WINTER LIGHT (Asylum, 1994)
- FEELS LIKE HOME (Asylum, 1995)
- DEDICATED TO THE ONE I LOVE (Elektra, 1996)
- WE RAN (Asylum, 1998)

Best of the "Best Of" Albums:
- GREATEST HITS (Asylum, 1976)
- GREATEST HITS, VOL. 2 (Asylum, 1980)
- THE LINDA RONSTADT VOX SET (Asylum, 1999)

~ 41 ~
Carly Simon

In the early 1970's, a growing number of women were successfully contending as solo rock singers: Linda Ronstadt, Joni Mitchell and Carole King, among others. Carly Simon was among that group, and like these others, she'd had some experience in the business back in the 1960's before rising to prominence in the 70's. Through the songs that she's released, heavily in the 1970's and more sporadically since then, Simon displayed a talent for writing rock songs that extended beyond the typical love ballads and "view of a relationship"-type songs that were the norm for so many others. Instead, there was often a matter-of-fact sarcastic, or even calloused edge to her songs. It was her songwriting talent, combined with her smooth, silky vocals that made her one of the most successful women rockers of the 1970's.

Born on June 25, 1945 in New York, Carly teamed up with her sister Lucy as a singing duo at an early age and began playing folk clubs and campuses around the New York area the very early 1960's. They even released a single, *Winkin' Blinkin' and Nod* in April 1964, which reached No. 73 on the US charts. By 1965, however, Lucy had decided to get married, and Carly had moved to France. She returned the following year and began doing solo performances and was spotted by manager Albert Grossman, who thought he could turn her into the female version of another performer that he managed, Bob Dylan.

Although she agreed to sign with Grossman and recorded some tracks for an album, she quickly became disillusioned with his attempts to transform her image into one which she didn't feel suited her. She broke away from Grossman and spent the next four years working as a singer of jingles while working on demos and writing new material for herself with Jacob Brackman. In 1969 she met Jac Holzman, the founder of Elektra Records, and in 1970 she signed a deal with the label for an album.

The self-titled debut album was released in April 1971 and reached No. 20 on the US charts. It featured her first hit, *That's The Way I've Always Heard It Should Be*, which peaked at No. 10. Even with her first solo single it was evident that Simon's writing didn't center around protest songs or syrupy love songs, but rather songs dealing with the ironic and bitter edge that life and love can have, and this was the subject matter that continued to appear in her songs.

A second album, ANTICIPATION, followed in 1971, as did NO SECRETS in 1972. While ANTICIPATION had produced a hit with its title track, much more attention (and speculation) arose from the first hit from NO SECRETS, *You're So Vain*. The song became the topic of discussion not just with fans, but also for people in general at the water-coolers and at home. The song, a smack-in-the-face at the vanity of a former lover, kept many people guessing as to who Simon was singing about. She never did give up a name.

1974 saw the release of HOTCAKES, which featured a Top 10 version of *Mockingbird* with her then-husband James Taylor. It was followed in 1975 with the album PLAYING POSSUM, and ANOTHER PASSENGER in 1977, and then she sang the theme song for the James Bond movie THE SPY WHO LOVED ME in 1978. Every year produced a new album or single from Simon and nearly every album had at least one Top 40 single, including the uncredited vocals on *Kissing with Confidence* in 1983.

By the mid-1980's, Simon had begun to slow down and her albums starting slipping down from the Top 40. She'd also stopped touring for the most part, particularly after a 1980 incident when she collapsed from exhaustion during a show in Pittsburgh, Pennsylvania. It led to an increasing dread of audiences and she found herself wanting to spend more time working on writing projects (including some children's books that were published). Additional complications in the 1990's from a bout with cancer also slowed her down. Even so, Carly Simon has released something new every 2 or 3 years since then and has a new album coming out in 2000 called THE BEDROOM TAPES. As always, her fans can't wait.

Selected Studio Albums:
- CARLY SIMON (Elektra, 1971)
- ANTICIPATION (Elektra, 1971)
- NO SECRETS (Elektra, 1972)
- HOTCAKES (Elektra, 1974)
- PLAYING POSSUM (Elektra, 1975)
- ANOTHER PASSENGER (Elektra, 1976)
- TAKIN' IT EASY (Warner Brothers, 1977)
- BOYS IN THE TREES (Elektra, 1978)
- SPY (Elektra, 1979)
- COME UPSTAIRS (Warner Brothers, 1980)
- TORCH (Warner Brothers, 1981)
- HELLO BIG MAN (Warner Brothers, 1983)
- SPOILED GIRL (Epic, 1985)
- COMING AROUND AGAIN (Arista, 1987)

- ○ MY ROMANCE (Arista, 1990)
- ○ HAVE YOU SEEN ME LATELY (Arista, 1990)
- ○ THIS IS MY LIFE (Qwest, 1992)
- ○ ROMULUS HUNT — A FAMILY OPERA (Angel, 1993)
- ○ LETTERS NEVER SENT (Arista, 1994)
- ○ FILM NOIR (Arista, 1997)
- ○ THE BEDROOM TAPES (Arista, 2000)

Best of the "Best Of" Albums:
- ○ THE BEST OF CARLY SIMON (Elektra, 1975)
- ○ CLOUDS IN MY COFFEE 1966 — 1996 (Arista, 1995)
- ○ THE VERY BEST OF CARLY SIMON (Warner Brothers, 1998)

~ 42 ~
Siouxsie Sioux

In the late 1970's a style of songwriting appeared that was unique to women songwriters — poetic mysticism. It was obvious in the work of Patti Smith in the mid-70's and grew with the highly successful writing soon after of writer / performers such as Stevie Nicks and Kate Bush. They were serious and sometimes dark tales of people in realms that were not quite that of our world. Sometimes of ghosts, sometimes of longing, sometimes of things that lurked so deep in the subconscious that it would be hard at times to even really say exactly what drew one to these songs. In the works of both Kate Bush and Stevie Nicks, there's a feeling of ultimate optimism. In fact, if we were to be so presumptuous as to suggest stereotypes for these two performers, you could say they were like the white witches of rock.

To counterbalance the white, there had to be darkness as well. Siouxsie Sioux came out of the punk movement of the mid-1970's and seemed top draw poetic dark magic out of the air with her songs. She was the counterpoint to the light and happy offerings of other performers. She was the dark witch, and the magic in her songs wove a spell that still lingers in her newest work, and in the music of other performers who were influenced by her. She was there at the threshold of punk in the 1970's, and one of the early innovators of the goth movement that was to follow, although trying to fit her into the mold of either would severely limit her accomplishments.

Born Susan Ballion (sometimes incorrectly listed in biographies as Dallion) in London, England on May 27, 1957, she was working as a waitress when she became gripped by the rising tide of the punk movement in 1976. Thanks to bands like the Ramones, the punk movement had begun to grow in the London area, having already rooted itself in other areas of the UK and in isolated parts of the US. With total abandon, and often minimal musical skill, it wasn't unlikely to find a band jumping on stage to play a show with little or no rehearsal. All that mattered was the willingness and ability to get up on stage and Do It Yourself.

It was in this atmosphere that Ballion on vocals, Marco Pirroni (who later enjoyed success performing and writing with Adam Ant) on guitar, Steve Severin (then known as Steve Havoc) on bass and Sid Vicious (yes, *that* Sid Vicious) on drums decided to perform live at the 100 Club's Punk Festival on September 20, 1976. To do the gig, they decided on a name that was one part horror movie (specifically, CRY OF THE BANSHEE, an early 1970's horror movie starring Vincent Price) and one part variation of Susan's name. Wanting to stay with her name, but knowing that being called "Susie" was hardly synonymous with the breaking punk movement, Ballion instead went with a spelling variation (based on the Sioux Indian Tribe) and elected to be "Siouxsie Sioux" in the band. Thus, Siouxsie and the Banshees were born.

Not that it was an easy birth. The band's first gig consisted of a 20 minute long recitation of *The Lord's Prayer* that remained long in the audience's memories (who could've imagined that someone would actually do a 20 minute version of *The Lord's Prayer*) and the band split up immediately afterward. Severin and Siouxsie, however, decided to stick it out and by July 1977 they had put together a firm lineup with Kenny Morris on drums and John McKay on guitar. After nearly another year of playing opening gigs and a radio session for John Peel, they were signed to Polydor Records in June 1978. Their first single, *Hong Kong Garden* reached the Top 10 on the UK charts, and was quickly followed by a major tour in October 1978 and the release of their first album in December, THE SCREAM (which reached No. 12 on the UK charts).

1979 brought continuing success with the release of two UK Top 30 singles (*The Staircase Mystery* and *Playground Twist*) and the album JOIN HANDS, which reached No. 13 on the UK charts. But trouble came in September of that year when both McKay and Morris dropped out of the band on the second night of a major promotional tour. Anxious to continue the tour, Severin and Sioux were able to obtain the services of Robert Smith from the Cure and Budgie (who had worked with The Slits). While Smith would be an on-again / off-again presence in the band because his commitment to The Cure, Budgie not only became a permanent fixture in the Banshees, but also teamed with Siouxsie in a project called The Creatures (more about which later). He also became romantically involved with Siouxsie, leading to their marriage in 1991.

Although JOIN HANDS still had punk music traces reminiscent of the first album, it was evident that their musical style was already starting to change. This was a breakout moment for the band — in 1978 the punk movement was already starting to converge solely into Sex Pistols-wannabes, trashing social icons with little musical direction, looking only to make the quickest gimmick-spawned buck. Instead, The Banshees were already progressing into a

courtesy Hot Wacks

style of dance music mixed with a darker lyrical image that was in evidence in the Romantics period of the early 1980's and finally formed the roots of the Goth movement of the mid-to-late 1980's. It was even more in evident with their next album, KALEDIOSCOPE, which featured John McGeoch replacing Robert Smith and reached No. 5 on the UK charts.

Siouxsie's image was also transforming. From the early days of punk-shock-values (when she wore a swastika armband, which she later admitted regretting, and exposed her breasts on stage) she had metamorphosed to more of a new wave look by the time of JOIN HANDS. That had changed even further with the release of JUJU in March 1981. Siouxsie transformed her clothing style into a more conservative, antique look, complete with lace and fineries, consisting of black, reds and other dark colors. Along with this came what became Siouxsie's trademark, her makeup, including the rather riveting use of eyeliner and eyeshadow that transformed her eyes into dark wells peering into her soul.

With the JUJU's reliance on lyrics that sometimes read as adult fairy tales (including a song that The Banshees are probably best remembered for, *Spellbound*) and Siouxsie's unique visual style, it was no wonder that the band became immensely popular. Some would even say that Siouxsie became a fashion icon for girls and women looking to strip away the sunny disposition perpetuated by other popular stars, particularly those of the early-to-mid 1980's such as Cyndi Lauper and Madonna. People who simply liked her looks and had never heard her albums were buying Siouxsie posters and T-shirts. In a sense, she became an anti-social pin-up girl.

Which, again, would have probably made Siouxsie less than thrilled. And for every appearance at which she appeared in her trademark attire and makeup, there were just as many appearances without them. There was no real rhyme or reason to her well-known dress code — it was just something to wear and it seemed to work. What was more important was that the music was being played and people were listening.

In fact, the musical side was going so well, that Budgie and Siouxsie undertook a project outside of The Banshees in October 1981 to record their first single together under the name The Creatures. While it may have seemed odd to record outside of the commercially successful Banshees, it certainly didn't hurt, and *Mad-Eyed Screamers* reached the Top 30 in the UK.

A compilation album appeared in early 1982, and the band finally released a new album in November of that year called A KISS IN THE DREAMHOUSE. With its success, Polydor agreed to setup a label for the group, and the new year saw the release of two albums on the Wonderland label: The Creatures album, FEAST, and an album called LIKE AN ANIMAL done by Severin, Robert Smith and Jeanette Landray under the name Glove. By this time, Smith had returned to the Banshees (replacing McGeoch) and would stay with them through the release of their double live album, NOCTURNE in December 1983.

HYENA was released in 1984, continuing the thread of darkly danceable music. Meanwhile, Smith once again left the band, this time to be replaced by John Carruthers. The Banshees visual style took root in their music videos, and with the band finally getting a domestic US release through Geffen, they began to get some recognition in the

States beyond the fans of the local alternative radio stations. They followed up their breakthrough in the US by touring there in 1986, which helped their 1986 album, TINDERBOX, to reach the US Top 100.

IN 1987 the band took a break, releasing of an album of cover songs, THROUGH THE LOOKING GLASS. With this record came another change in the band's lineup, with John Klein replacing Carruthers and Martin McCarrick joining on keyboards. This would be the last change in their lineup until 1995 when McCarrick and Klein would leave.

1988 saw the release of PEEPSHOW, and the critical praise for the album had them moving in a startlingly new direction with an emphasis on a techno-pop dance style. Which just shows that the critics hadn't been listening to the band's earlier material. Although there were certainly songs that were melodic and orchestrated (such as *Cities In Dust* or their revamped version of the Beatles' *Dear Prudence*), and those songs whose focus had psychedelic underpinnings, there had always been a good number of tracks with a strong dance beat (probably Budgie's influence in the songwriting) and Siouxsie's music has always been remarkably danceable. It was more a case of the critics and record label representatives wanting to pigeonhole the band so as to satisfy their own belief

courtesy Hot Wacks

in what was sellable, and in so doing demonstrated how little understanding of the music they actually had.

PEEPSHOW didn't do quite as well as earlier albums, and Siouxsie and Budgie followed up the album with another Creatures release, BOOMERANG, in March 1990, going so far as to tour for the album in the US. This was followed by the June 1991 release of the Banshee album SUPERSTITION and the hit single *Kiss Them For Me*.

Time was spent on other outside projects between studio albums after 1991, with TWICE UPON A TIME — THE SINGLES being released in 1992, and a few singles released between 1992 through 1995. The band returned in 1995 with the album THE RAPTURE, but 1996 was pretty much the end of the road.

1996 was the twenty year mark since the explosion of the punk movement. Long gone, but hardly forgotten (and fondly remembered by far too many people who never lived through it), it seemed like a perfect opportunity for many to cash in on, including the Sex Pistols reuniting for a tour. For Siouxsie, it was the return of a rotting corpse and a time that she hadn't held on to; one, in fact, that she'd firmly left behind by 1978-79.

But that made little difference to the press and the critics. To them, Siouxsie and the Banshees were a success story of the punk movement, and because of the cynical revival of 1996, the band was uniformly stereotyped as just another nostalgia act. It didn't seem to matter that Siouxsie had progressed beyond those years; it didn't matter that they'd been recording continuously and almost yearly since 1977; and it didn't matter that Siouxsie had played a major role in the development of several rock cultures — goth, punk and new wave — the Banshees were still being strung up as another old corpse for everyone to gawk at.

An that corpse was the death of the band. In 1996, after recording one more song that ended up on the soundtrack album of the dismal film, SHOWGIRLS (*New Skin*), Siouxsie announced the breakup of the band for good. In doing so, she directly cited the punk nostalgia as being a major contributor to the end of the band. Not wanting to be shoehorned into a role that she'd never held in the first place, it was better to bow out than to fight a useless battle.

Still, although The Banshees died, it wasn't the end of Siouxsie Sioux. Instead, she and Budgie continued with their work as The Creatures and released a new album in 1999 called ANIMA ANIMUS. They also toured in 1999 and there's no end in sight for new material from Siouxsie.

Never the one to follow the trends, Siouxsie Sioux continues on her own path. In doing so, she has managed to avoid titles being hung on her, although her work has shaped so much in the musical world that titles would be so easy to give.

Selected Studio albums (as part of Siouxsie and the Banshees):
   ◦ THE SCREAM (Polydor/Geffen, 1978)
   ◦ JOIN HANDS (Polydor/Geffen, 1979)
   ◦ KALEISOSCOPE (Polydor/Geffen, 1980)
   ◦ JUJU (Polydor/Geffen, 1981)
   ◦ A KISS IN THE DREAMHOUSE (Polydor/Geffen, 1982)
   ◦ HYAENA (Wonderland Records/Geffen, 1984; first album released under Geffen, all earlier albums reissued after 1984)
   ◦ TINDERBOX (Wonderland/Geffen, 1986)
   ◦ THROUGH THE LOOKING GLASS (Wonderland/Geffen, 1987)
   ◦ PEEPSHOW (Wonderland/Geffen, 1988)
   ◦ SUPERSTITION (Wonderland/Geffen, 1991)
   ◦ THE RAPTURE (Wonderland/Geffen, 1995)

Selected Studio Albums (as part of the Creatures):
   ◦ FEAST (Wonderland, 1983)

- ◦ BOOMERANG (Wonderland, 1989)
- ◦ ANIMA ANIMUS (Sioux, 1999)

Best of the "Best Of" Albums:
- ◦ ONCE UPON A TIME / THE SINGLES (Polydor/Geffen, 1981)
- ◦ TWICE UPON A TIME / THE SINGLES (Polydor/Geffen, 1992)

Live Albums:
- ◦ NOCTURNE (Geffen, 1983)

~ 43 ~
Grace Slick

If there was one singer who was the siren voice of the psychedelic 60's, it had to have been Grace Slick. Looking no further than the biggest hits — *Somebody To Love* and *White Rabbit* — of the band she helped front, Jefferson Airplane, should prove that to be the case. Not only that, but these songs have come to represent the music that's remembered of that period, often times used in soundtracks to purvey the unique period of drugs, mind-expanding awareness and the intellectual aspects of the whole hippie movement. With a voice whose intensity held a ragged edge, as if the words were final messages left behind by unworldly spirits, Slick shaped not only the success of the Airplane, but also (in writing *White Rabbit*) the memories of the era.

Born Grace Wing on October 30, 1939 in Chicago, Illinois, her early years were normal for that time and place. Growing up in Palo Alto, California, Grace eventually ended up in modeling and was doing so when she happened to go see a new band called Jefferson Airplane in 1965 with her husband Jerry Slick and his brother Darby. Seeing how the band was having so much fun performing on stage (and probably making better money for less work), Grace, Jerry and Darby decided to form their own band, which they called The Great Society. The band was beginning to get recognition and had started recording material when the Airplane found itself without a female vocalist (following the departure of Signe Anderson). When Grace was asked to join, she dropped out of The Great Society (and her marriage to Jerry Slick) to join the Airplane. Two things she did retain were her last name and two songs that had been written for The Great Society, *White Rabbit* and *Somebody to Love*.

Those two songs became Airplane's biggest hits and thrust Slick into the prominent role as the center of the band (much to the chagrin of fellow lead vocalist Marty Balin). The band continued on, with numerous changes over the next few years, but by 1973 the energy of the hippie movement, and popularity for their psychedelic and often political music, was at an all time low. Facing solo careers and splits into other bands, Jefferson Airplane broke up only to be resurrected within the year by Paul Kantner as Jefferson Starship.

Grace continued working with Kantner (sharing creative control along with a relationship that produced a daughter, China), and it was her voice that was the clear connection between the two bands. Their music took on a more otherworldly and science fiction-like flavor, moving away from the politics of early Airplane albums. Little did it matter to fans, who purchased the albums by the truckload and kept the band in the Top 10 album after album.

The 1960's gave Grace a freedom to explore and taste life on a larger level than most people dare to. Surprisingly, nothing seemed to effect her except for an older generation drug, alcohol, which lead to her missing some concerts for Jefferson Starship in 1978 and then her quitting the band at that time. She'd already done one solo album by that time and it was assumed that she would probably continue her solo work after splitting from Jefferson Starship. She did just that with her album DREAMS in 1980, followed by WELCOME TO THE WRECKING BALL in 1981. Since both albums did well on the charts for solo efforts, many were surprised when Slick then returned to Jefferson Starship.

Again, she shared vocal duties with a male singer, this time Mickey Thomas, and Jefferson Starship continued to have Top 10 hits during the first part of the 1980's. A steady change of emphasis in the band's music had come over the years, however, being increasingly geared towards love songs and plenty of them. This suited the duet nature of Slick and Thomas very well, but it was obvious that some of the band members — particularly Slick and Kantner — were seeing Jefferson Starship more and more as a commercial product and less as an artistic one. In 1985 Kantner left the band and threaten to sue them in order to have them drop the "Jefferson" part of their name. Thus, they became Starship. But that didn't stop them from continuing to put out hits, with Slick and Thomas right on top singing.

Slick went along with the deconstruction of the band, but by 1988 she'd realized that they were becoming a bunch of old men singing teenage love songs and pap pop. So she left and rejoined Kantner in a resurrected version of Jefferson Airplane. The revised Airplane went through several phases, but never quite got off the ground again, and Slick eventually pulled out, feeling it was time to move on.

1998 saw the release of Slick's autobiography, SOMEBODY TO LOVE?, which sold quite well and put her back into the limelight for a brief time. Even with the new attention, Grace seemed quite happy with her retirement — away from the rock scene and from the pressures attached to an image that was appropriate only for a younger woman. Besides, she'd made it through the decades still in one piece, having had the chance to enjoy the life that she'd set out to pursue — which makes her a success in life as well as in the world of Rock and Roll.

Studio Albums (as part of the Great Society):
- CONSPICUOUS ONLY IN ITS ABSENCE (Columbia, 1968)
- HOW IT WAS (Columbia, 1968)

Selected Studio Albums (as part of Jefferson Airplane):
- SURREALISTIC PILLOW (RCA, 1967)
- AFTER BATHING AT BAXTER'S (RCA, 1967)
- CROWN OF CREATION (RCA, 1968)
- BLESS ITS POINTED LITTLE HEAD (RCA, 1969)
- VOLUNTEERS (1969)
- BARK (Grunt, 1971)
- LONG JOHN SILVER (Grunt, 1972)

Selected Studio Albums (as part of Jefferson Starship):
- BLOWS AGAINST THE EMPIRE (RCA, 1970)
- DRAGON FLY (RCA, 1974)
- RED OCTOPUS (RCA, 1975)
- SPITFIRE (RCA, 1976)
- MODERN TIMES (RCA, 1981)
- WINDS OF CHANGE (RCA, 1983)
- NUCLEAR FURNITURE (RCA, 1984)

Selected Studio Albums (as part of Starship):
- KNEE DEEP IN THE HOOPLA (RCA, 1985)
- NO PROTECTION (RCA, 1987)

Selected Studio Albums:
- SUNFIGHTER (Grunt 1971 [with Kantner])
- BARON VON TOLLBOOTH AND THE CHROME NUN (Grunt, 1973 [with Kantner and David Freiberg])
- MANHOLE (Grunt, 1973)
- DREAMS (RCA, 1980)
- WELCOME TO THE WRECKING BALL (RCA, 1981)
- SOFTWARE (RCA, 1984)

Best of the "Best Of" Albums:
- THE WORST OF JEFFERSON AIRPLANE (RCA, 1970)
- JEFFERSON AIRPLANE LOVES YOU (RCA, 1990)
- GOLD (RCA, 1998)
- THE BEST OF GRACE SLICK (RCA, 1999)

Live Albums:
- THIRTY SECONDS OVER WINTERLAND (Grunt, 1983)

~ 44 ~
Patti Smith

Other artists have been referred to as the voice of their generation, or it's been said that their musical style depicts the zenith of their genre. References to Patti Smith have ranged from "the godmother of punk" to the first of the truly poetic writer of the Rock and Roll age. Rarely is she referred to as the voice for her generation. And as for being the zenith, well, while some fans are moved by her early work in HORSES and EASTER, those same fans are somewhat embarrassed to admit that they're also moved by her later work in GONE AGAIN and DREAM OF LIFE. To admit to liking both eras is to admit to a conflict in personal taste. But that's just the way it is — artists also progress through life.

Born December 30, 1946 in Chicago, Illinois, Patti grew up with her family in a variety of locations, including Paris, London, New Jersey and New York. While raised as a Jehovah's Witness (her mother's faith), by the age of 12 she'd decided that she wanted to become an painter and had moved away from her religious training to concentrate on her career. Along with painting, she also turned to writing, especially poetry, and starting working to have her poems published. In 1969 she began writing professionally for Rock magazine (she would also later write for Creem), but by the next year she was already trying out her poetry in public outings. Meeting up with fellow critic Lenny Kaye, she asked him to accompany her readings on guitar and this was the seed that grew into the music Smith began to write in 1970.

By 1974 she had put together a more structure band, which was still centered around her poetry readings, and her first single, *Piss Factory* was released that year. It was a small release, and controversial to say the least, but Sire Records eventually picked it up for national distribution and the Patti Smith Group was soon to become a well-known name.

Her first full length album, HORSES, was released in 1975 and received high critical praise for its anxious and dark lyrics and Smith's unique singing style. She next traveled to Europe to tour in 1976 (helping push the punk movement into place over there), and was came back to the US to release RADIO ETHIOPIA in December 1976. This album was another critical success, and her fans began to trust Smith to produce high quality material on each album, but it didn't do as well as HORSES on the charts. Things changed with her next album, EASTER, which featured her first Top 20 hit, *Because The Night*, co-written by Bruce Springsteen (it was the first Top 20 hit that Springsteen had contributed to as well). The album reached No. 20 on the US charts and Smith soon became an icon of the early punk movement.

Not that she really wanted to be anyone's icon. After the release of her next album, WAVE, she married Fred Smith (formerly of the MC5, another band considered to be a forerunner of punk) and left the rock world until 1988 when she released her next album DREAM OF LIFE. This album, done hand-in-hand with Fred, was a surprise for those fans who had wondered what happened to Patti. The material on the album was also a surprise, being more upbeat and personal than her earlier recordings.

But DREAM OF LIFE wasn't Patti's full return to the Rock and Roll world. It was another seven years before her next album, GONE AGAIN was released, another album of personal poetry dealing with the passing of her husband in 1994. GONE AGAIN, started with Fred earlier in 1994, showed Smith progressing toward a more sedate, yet still tough and determined, view of life and the sharing of life with others. If DREAM OF LIFE had thrown some of the old fans, GONE AGAIN did even more so. But many fans accepted that it was a stretch into another area of her poetry and the album was nearly universally praised as a return of Smith in good form.

Smith continued to perform on a semi-regular basis after that, producing another album in 1997, PEACE AND NOISE, and another in 2000 with GUNG HO. Despite all of the professional and critical praise for Smith's work over the years, it's never been tagged as being of one particular genre. Even though she's sometimes looked upon as a predecessor of punk music in the early 1970's, she's rarely referred to as a punk artist. Nor will you find many fans that would be able to say, "Patti's music speaks for my generation." Which is just as well, since locking her work into one mode would have been the stifling of her creativity. It's quite simply the work of an artist with her own point of view, and a shape and tone of both the lyrics and the music have changed over time. When an artist continues to develop and can't be pinned down, that's usually when the true innovations in music appear. Patti refuses to be pinned down.

Selected Studio Albums:
- HORSES (Arista, 1975)
- RADIO ETHIOPIA (Arista, 1976)
- EASTER (Arista, 1978)
- SET FREE (Arista, 1978)
- WAVE (Arista, 1979)
- DREAM OF LIFE (Arista, 1988)
- GONE AGAIN (Arista, 1996)
- PATTI SMITH (Arista, 1997)
- PEACE AND NOISE (Arista, 1997)
- GUNG HO (Arista, 2000)

Best of the "Best Of" Albums:
- PATTI SMITH: BOX SET (RCA, 1991)

~ 45 ~
Patty Smyth

The early 1980's saw a large number of bands emerge in the wake of the new wave movement and the beginning of the music video revolution on MTV. The atmosphere was ripe not only for bands to be visually entertaining (the music videos), but the new wave movement helped spark a return to straight forward pop rock instead the heavy orchestrations of the late 1970's rock music and the chaos of the punk movement. More so, it returned "power pop" to the tool boxes of musicians as an acceptable musical genre. There were a variety of bands that also came fronted by women singers during this period, ranging from the smoky love songs of the Motels, to the techno-beats of Missing Persons. Many came and went quickly, some stuck it out for awhile. In some cases that was just as well, but sometimes it was a shame to see some of the impressive talent disappear.

Scandal was one of the bands that emerged during this period and their lead singer was Patty Smyth. Smyth was born in New York City on June 26, 1957 with a musical background pretty much unavoidable thanks to her mother running a club in the New York area. The club catered to the folk music scene for a time, but as the 1970's came on, switched to rock music and Smyth was undoubtedly exposed to a lot of the bands that would later start the punk and new wave movements.

Embarking on a career as a singer, Smyth heard about a band being started by Zack Smith, a guitarist wanting to start his own group after playing in a variety of other bands, including ones that featured Dee Murray and Davey Johnson of Elton John's band. Smith was looking to put together a band that had a slight new wave edge, but had more of a "power pop" feel and decided to call the band Scandal. With connections already available to the band, they began their career opening up for other artists on the road and developing their style there before recording their first single, the excellent *Goodbye to You* in 1982.

The single was a massive hit, especially after receiving airplay on the brand-new (at the time) music channel MTV. Thanks to the success of that video (as well as a video for *Love Has a Line on You*), the album raced up the charts and the band was on their way.

While Scandal's music was a definite reason for their success, there was no denying the fact that Smyth's vocals were a major factor as well. A clear, youthful singing voice, backed with just a touch of a ragged edge to give it some roughness, it became a prototype for the singing style that would be in vogue for much of the 1980's.

Because of her singing abilities and her position as frontman of the group, most of the attention drawn to the band was directed at Patty. By the time the follow-up album, THE WARRIOR, came out in 1984, they had changed from simply Scandal, to "Scandal, featuring Patty Smyth." It was a Platinum-selling album, but as is the case with most bands where one member was elevated to part of the band's name, they split within the year.

Smyth followed the split by putting out her first solo album in 1987, NEVER ENOUGH. It featured a few hits, including a duet with Don Henley called *Sometimes Love Just Ain't Enough*, which hit No. 2. Yet,

Smyth found other personal projects more to her liking and she didn't complete another album until 1992, called simply PATTY SMYTH. This album didn't do as well as her first and she withdrew even further from recording. Since then, there has been some talk of Smyth returning to the studios to record another album, but she has essentially stated that she has other thing she wants to do.

Patty Smyth represents one of the best voices to come out of the early 1980's, but her story also represents what all too often happened to performers from that period. It's a shame, because her vocals are a great memory of the period and it would be nice to think that more material from her will be out there some day.

Studio Albums (as part of Scandal):
- ° SCANDAL (Columbia, 1982)
- ° THE WARRIOR (Columbia, 1984)

Solo Selected Studio Albums:
- ° NEVER ENOUGH (Columbia, 1987)
- ° PATTY SMYTH (MCA, 1992)

~ 46 ~
Ronnie Spector

The girl-groups were an aspect of Rock and Roll music that stood out as a sub-genre all on their own. Not that people don't sometimes have trouble keeping all the girl-groups straight (or thinking that there was only one). It may have started off in the early days of recording as a variation of the choir or chorus sing, but by the early 1960's there were dozens of girl-groups like the Crystals, the Supremes, the Angels, the Chiffons and the Shirelles. Within a few years some of girl-groups picked up guitars themselves and become the band, thus cutting out the middleman. But in the early 1960's, being in a girl-group was one of the few options for a woman who wanted to sing Rock and Roll.

Among the girl-groups, there were a few voices that stood out. One singer, who was the focus of the Ronettes and sang some of the biggest girl-group songs ever recorded, was Ronnie Spector. Her vocal style had a piercing clarity that even Phil Spector's Wall of Sound couldn't distort or cover up completely. It was and is a voice that could never be quite duplicated.

Born Veronica Bennett on August 10, 1947 in New York, Ronnie grew up wanting to be a singer. She wanted it so badly, in fact, that she convince her sister Estelle and her cousin Nedra Talley to sing with her, and for her mother to help pay for singing lessons for the trio. Starting out by singing at bar mitzvahs as the Darling Sisters, they later changed their stage name to Ronnie and the Relatives. In 1961 the group had gained enough experience through sockhops and bar mitzvahs that they finally had a chance to audition for Stu Phillips at Colpix Records. Given the chance, they recorded several songs for the label overr the next several months, but little came of the singles when they were released. Instead, the group tried its luck at the Peppermint Lounge, which at the time was the hottest rock music club in the New York.

Given an opportunity to dance for the audience, Ronnie took a chance by singing *What'd I Say?* when she was jokingly given the microphone during a Joey Dee and the Starlighters set at the club. When the song went over well, the club owner decided they were good enough to sing a couple of songs each night. With that opportunity, they changed their name one last time — to the Ronettes.

The gigs at the Peppermint Lounge led to working for Murray the K (the famous New York DJ) as backing singers and dancers for several acts during in his revues. The Ronettes started to become known around the area, but none of the singles ever moved. That is, until Phil Spector came along in 1963. Or rather, that the Ronettes came along for Phil Spector.

Knowing already (in 1963) what Spector was capable of, and knowing that he had worked successes for the Crystals, Ronnie and Estelle got up the nerve to contact Spector to see if he was interested in giving them an audition. Fortunately, they reached him and, fortunately, he was interested in hearing them audition. As it turned out, Spector not only loved Ronnie's voice for its uniqueness, but was also taken by Ronnie as a person. Although he was solely interested in Ronnie, he was convinced by Ronnie's mother to sign the complete group. After a brief delay to get out of their Colpix contract, Spector began working with the Ronettes.

Their first single, *Be My Baby*, became the group's biggest hit. It was also the song that signaled one of the zeniths of the whole girl group phenomena, and it was Ronnie's voice that made it all possible. From there, Spector continued working with the group and the Ronettes had many more hits. Their popularity increased to the point that they were opening for some of the hottest bands of the 1960's — the Beatles and the Rolling Stones. In some ways, the Ronettes were the center of attention when it came to girl-groups (although some would argue that the Surpremes held that position). The only problem was that their subsequent hits were never quite as big as the first one. Also, as time went on, the public's interest in Spector's brand of production was waning.

Still things were very good for Ronnie in the early 1960's and she and Phil eventually married, after having become closer during those years. As it was, however, the closeness led to the two almost disappearing for a time, which wasn't a good thing for the active and personable Ronnie. As Spector's interests closed in (because of the disinterest of the American public for his production of Tina Turner's version of *River Deep, Mountain High*) and he became more reclusive, Ronnie found herself unable to display her talents, choosing instead to stand by Phil during this time away from the spotlight. The Ronettes virtually disappeared after 1965, reemerging in 1969 for a short time. The reunion didn't last long and it wasn't until Ronnie finally left Phil in 1973 that she began to appear in public again, singing and dancing.

courtesy Hot Wacks

Since that time, Ronnie has recorded several songs that deserved to be hits, especially those with artists like The E Street Band and Joey Ramone of the Ramones, but for some bizarre reason the songs never made it up the charts. Beyond that, Ronnie has found herself a niche as a singer in clubs and enjoys performing for the crowds who are always interested in hearing her sing again.

Ronnie had one huge hit after the 1960's ended, with Eddie Money — a singer who was also making a bit of a comeback in 1986 with his song *Take Me Home Tonight*. The song featured a reference to Ronnie and *Be My Baby*, and it was suggested that maybe they could get Ronnie for the vocals. When asked if she would be interested in singing the part herself, Ronnie said yes, and it is her happy and sparkling vocals that can be heard singing those few words that caught so much attention back in 1963.

And the passing years hadn't made any difference. Her voice was as strong as ever. It was a genuine joy to hear her voice and behold her face after that many years and see that sometimes time really does stand still.

Selected Studio Albums (as part of the Ronettes):
- CHRSTMAS GIFT (Phillies, 1963)
- PRESENTING THE FABULOUS RONETTES (Phillies, 1964)
- THE RONETTES (Colpix, 1965)

Best of the "Best Of" Albums:
- THE RONETTES: THE EARLY YEARS (Rhino, 1990)
- THE BEST OF THE RONETTES (ABKCO, 1992)

Selected Studio Albums:
- SIREN (Polish, 1980)
- UNFINISHED BUSINESS (Columbia, 1987)
- DANGEROUS (Raven, 1996)
- SHE TALKS TO RAINBOWS (Kill Rock Star, 1999)

~ 47 ~
Dusty Springfield

The world changes over time as opinions and fads shift and the mood of the people quickly turns from one idea of what is popular to another. As people change, they sometimes end up creating a false dislike for material that they had loved just months or even weeks before, only to eventually come back years later to look upon those early loves and wonder why they had turned against them. Unfortunately, rediscovery of those old loves usually comes too late benefit to the artists who gave us their all and then struggled once we turned away.

That was almost the story of Dusty Springfield. Not quite, since renewed recognition came her way nearly two decades later, but even then the happy ending we would hope for didn't come about.

Dusty Springfield was born Mary Isabel Catherine Bernadette O'Brien on April 16, 1939 in Hampstead, London, England. Growing up in a household that included music as diverse as classical and jazz, Dusty began her singing career as part of a vocal trio called the Lana Sisters. After recording a few singles with the group, she eventually left to join her brother Dion and a friend of his named Tim Field (later replaced in 1962 by Mike Pickworth) to form a folk trio in 1960 called The Springfields. To complete the transformation, the trio began using "Springfield" as their surname, leading to Dusty's stage name that remained with her for the rest of her life.

The Springfields became so popular that they were not only a top-selling group in the UK, but also managed to break into the US charts with the song *Silver Threads and Golden Needles*. As a result, the trio toured the US and Dusty became fascinated by the Motown movement, just then beginning to take off in the states. Wanting to move beyond the folk sound that had been her success, Dusty decided to branch out from the trio and try a solo career. The Springfields broke up in September 1963 and Dusty signed a deal with Philips in the UK.

It was a remarkable break that The Sprinfields has enjoyed success so early in their career, and it became even more remarkable when Dusty's first solo single, the soul-influenced *I Only Want to Be With You*, broke through on both the UK and US charts. From there, there was no stopping Dusty's rocketing career and it seemed as if every song she recorded was guaranteed to do well on both sides of the ocean. Her sound was a mixture of the soulful rock music being made at Motown in the states with a strong touch of the European cabaret style, and Dusty's vocal abilities turned every song into a powerful vocal statement. Looking at her later hit, *Son of a Preacher Man*, we see that she not only understood the dynamics of the sound, but could also develop a storyline throughout the course of a song. In the hands of another artist, the song would have been a statement made outside of the storyline, perhaps that of a bad girl looking back at her fall. Instead, Dusty turned the track into a story, beginning with sweet innocence, and gradually becoming harder and more fulfilling as the song builds to its climax. By doing so, the song seems more to be a willing sexual conquest by the girl than just another story of a girl gone bad.

And it was this type of influence on her music that kept fans coming back for more over the years. It led to tours in both the US and UK, and top selling albums and singles in both countries as well. It even led to a short-run television series in the UK.

But it also led to Dusty beginning to second-guess herself. Always mapping her own ways even from the days of the Springfields, she was well-known for being demanding in the studios. She demanded a certain sound with her recordings and her vocals that sometimes even she felt she could not live up to, and it was an aggressive stance that turned some people away from working with her, marking her as difficult. For the most part, at that point in the 1960's, it didn't make much of a difference to her, just as long as the sound she wanted was there for people to hear when they bought her next record.

But times were changing. The situation where a singer could work on material and reshape songs into their own personal statements was becoming a thing of the past by the late 1960's. Instead, songwriters working outside of a band or otherwise being other than only a performer where beginning to be looked upon as hack performers, at least in the pop music world. With the success of the Beatles, who wrote a majority of their own material, most performers making waves in pop music were known for writing material "in-house" and not looking for outside writers. Dusty, on the other hand, worked best when taking work written by others and reshaping it to her own voice.

More importantly, the days of women singing ballads (even the rocking ones that Dusty and others did) were at an end by the late 1960's. For female singers, fans were turning to people like Joan Baez or Janis Joplin — voices that sang with a force rather than as a narrator of a story. 1970 saw Dusty's last Top 100 single for for nearly twenty years, with only three more songs reaching with the Top 100 in the UK during that period. Other women rockers in the same wave of popularity as Dusty during the early to mid-1960's were in the same fix, but some had other avenues to pursue. Petula Clark had an established acting career both before and after the 1960's, while Lesley Gore managed to

use her writing credits as a means to show her professional progress and returned to doing shows based on her earlier hits. Even Brenda Lee had further success by returning to her first love, country music. For Dusty, it was different. Her career was based on the type of music she was creating in the studios. With the shift in public tastes, she found herself set adrift with no direction.

Dusty tried to carry on with albums and singles through the 1970's which gained considerable critical acclaim, but went nowhere on the charts. To Dusty, it was devastating, and only further made her withdraw within herself as each new direction attempted hit a brick wall. By late 1970's, she had developed a reputation for being difficult, and was having problems with substance-abuse. Even if such problems where short-lived or simple misunderstandings, they did little to help her career and by 1983 she had cut herself back to recording only a handful of singles and little else. Because of her demanding where her own talents were concerned, she became susceptible to the idea that she was failing herself and withdrew even further.

Until 1987. The Pet Shop Boys, a UK techno-pop group who had found success, as had Dusty on both sides of the Atlantic, had requested Dusty to record a song with them called *What Have I Done To Deserve This?*. The song hit No. 2 in both the US and the UK and renewed the interest of Dusty's older fans and gained new fans that had never heard of her in the late 1980's (some of whom probably weren't even born at the time of her early hits). She followed up the success with a new album released in 1990 called REPUTATION, which returned her to the charts and the good graces of the public.

By 1995 she had recorded her last album, A VERY FINE LOVE, and had become recognized as a pioneering voice in pop vocals with her ability to project so much more into a song with than "just singing." She was a master storyteller, and an influential singer for many women vocalists who came after, particularly those who went on to record the same type of soulful music that was her first love back in the early 1960's.

Soon after the release of her final album, she admitted publicly that breast cancer, that she had previously undergone treatment for, had returned. Within three years she succumbed to cancer, passing away on March 2, 1999. Before she went, however, she received an OBE from the Queen and knew that she was set to be inducted into the Rock and Roll Hall of Fame.

Solo Selected Studio Albums:
- A GIRL CALLED DUSTY (Philips, 1964)
- DUSTY (Philips, 1964)
- OOOOOOWEEEE!!! (Philips, 1964)
- YOU DON'T HAVE TO SAY YOU LOVE ME (Philips, 1966)
- WHERE AM I GOING (Philips, 1967)
- THE LOOK OF LOVE (Philips, 1967)
- DUSTY DEFINITELY (Philips, 1968)
- DUSTY IN MEMPHIS (Philips, 1969; reissues with many additional tracks in 1999 by Rhino)
- A BRAND NEW ME (Philips, 1970)

- THIS IS DUSTY SPRINGFIELD (Philips, 1971)
- SEE ALL HER FACES (Philips, 1972)
- CAMEO (Dunhill, 1983)
- SINGS BACHARACH & KING (Philips, 1975)
- IT BEGINS AGAIN (Mercury, 1978)
- LIVING WITHOUT YOUR LOVE (Mercury, 1978)
- WHITE HEAT (Casablanca, 1983)
- REPUTATION (Alex, 1991)
- A VERY FINE LOVE (Columbia, 1995)

Best of the "Best Of" Albums:
- THE SILVER COLLLECTION (Philips, 1988)
- THE VERY BEST OF DUSTY SPRINGFIELD (Polygram, 1998)
- 20TH CENTURY MASERS — THE MILLENNIUM COLLECTION (Polygram, 1999)

~ 48 ~
Tina Turner

There are many women rock performers who are known for their musical abilities, creativity or individuality. But if there's one singer who is a symbol of the ability to stand alone and survive in rock music, the name that instantly comes to mind is Tina Turner. Sure, some would say that Tina's music is pure pop, or soul, or (like her early material with Ike) R&B, but that doesn't make her any less of a icon in the Rock and Roll world. Faced with career slumps, indifferent public reactions, and the record labels at times abusing and mocking her, Tina has shown an ability to face the world head-on. In doing so, she knocked them cold with a smile, a look, a strut and a voice such that they had to either bow down or move out of the way. And if rock is supposed to roll you over, an army would only need Tina to clear the way.

Born Annie Mae Bullock in Brownsville, Tennessee (although raised in Nutbush, Tennessee) on November 26, 1939, Tina grew up in a small sharecropper community full of hard days and rare chances to enjoy life. Raised by her grandmother, Tina sang in the church choir as she was growing up. The choir was the only outlet for her singing until a few years later when fate interceded. With the passing of her grandmother, Tina's mother took her and her sister, Alline, after the funeral, back to East St. Louis, only to leave them to struggle on their own in the city.

Working in East St. Louis, the sisters got to know the R&B clubs around town and it was in one of these clubs during 1956 that fate changed everything for Annie. Performing there was a well-known guitarist, Ike Turner (who had recorded a song in 1951considered by many to be one of the first Rock and Roll songs ever, *Rocket 88*), with his band The Kings of Rhythm, an act that Annie had seen before. Wanting to perform for the audience herself, Annie had offered to audition for Ike, but he showed little interest. Finally, grabbing at an opportunity to get the microphone one night, Tina

began singing for the audience and got an enthusiastic response from not only the audience and the band, but from Ike as well.

It was enough to convince Ike Turner to add Annie to the band as a vocalist, with a change in name from Annie to Tina (and the addition of Turner as a last name, even though Ike and Tina were not married until a few years later). Changing the band's name to the Ike and Tina Turner Revue, they continued playing a strong mixture of R&B and rock, with the rock sound becoming more prominent as Rock and Roll emerged as a power to be reckoned with during the 1960's. Within four years of meeting, Ike and Tina hit the R&B charts with the song *A Fool in Love*, and throughout the next 15 years they continued to ride that chart while also hitting the Top Ten charts in many other countries around the world. They finally hit the Top Ten rock charts in the US with a cover of *Proud Mary* in 1971.

With Ike's guitar methods and Tina's throaty, husky voice, it was no wonder that the band was doing so well around the world, especially in rock circles. There was an alluring "bad girl" quality to Tina's voice that made everything sound like there was a lot of personal truth in whatever she sang, and Ike had some first rate guitar licks. But that was just the icing on the cake when it came to seeing them live. Not only was the band animated, but Tina offered something that was very unusual for a women singer in the 1960's (and even in the 1970's) — she moved.

Most singers at the time stood in one place and perhaps shuffled a bit in a meager attempt at dancing, but that wasn't Tina's style. She was all over the place; and with the Ikettes backing her up on vocals, there were high-kicking, hip-shaking moves for everyone to see. Tina was a rare example of spectacular showmanship on stage during those days, with a visual style matched by no other woman singer out there (and rarely by male performers either). Her movements had flash and reached out to the center of what rock music was about — the dancing, the singing, the actions. Tina became the center of the stage show, while Ike remained the creative center of the act on record. It worked. And from all appearances, things were going well for everyone involved. At least it appeared that way.

Behind the scenes, however, things were not going well. Because of Ike's abuse and his worsening drug habit, the band was slowly dissolving, with members leaving left and right, while others struggled against each other to get what they could out of the band. Meanwhile, Tina had to face the abuse personally, trying her best to do what she could to keep her sanity. But by 1974 she'd had enough, and left Ike during the first part of a tour.

She took nothing professional or financial away from the years they'd had to together, refusing to contest Ike for money or profits in the divorce proceedings that took place in 1976. Instead, Tina spent time starting from scratch, playing clubs and making special appearances in Europe (where Ike and Tina had found more popularity in the 1960's than in the US). She even made a lively appearance in the movie version of the Who's TOMMY (playing the Acid Queen, thereby creating probably the most frightening facial creature on the face of the planet).

It was obviously a struggle. Not only had Tina faced physical and emotional problems with Ike, but also her professional life had been stuck in a "where are they now" file by the public in the US. Her style of outlandish outfits and high-kicking dancing had even been parodied on SATURDAY NIGHT LIVE, and her public appearances had been reduced to toothpaste commercials. Still, she carried on, determined to show that she could again achieve the success that the team of Ike and Tina once enjoyed.

By 1983, the struggle had begun to pay off. Thanks to some inducement by David Bowie, Capitol Records signed Tina to a record deal and released a cover version of Al Green's *Let's Stay Together* as her first single. It reached No. 6 on the UK charts, while breaking the Top 40 in the US. It was more than enough for Capitol, and a full album was produced for Tina and she began to tour the UK. The album was PRIVATE DANCER, and it became the biggest album of her career.

PRIVATE DANCER featured *What's Love Got To Do With It?*, which hit No. 1 in the US (her first No. 1 song on the US Pop charts, even when she was with Ike). The album's title track followed it, also doing well in the charts. The album itself hit No. 3 in the US (selling 5 million in the US alone).

It was a rebirth in the public's awareness of Tina Turner, and she made no qualms about being in control of the audience that she now had listening to and watching her. She followed up PRIVATE DANCER with extensive touring and she received the respect of both her audiences and other professionals in the business with every step she took.

Since that time, Tina has produced a series of studio albums that haven't quite matched the sales of PRIVATE DANCER, but she's become one of the few women rockers who can consistently fill arenas and stadiums for her shows. She's been compared to the likes of stage-grabbing performers like David Bowie and Mick Jagger in concert — a feat that only few can claim. She's also continued to prove that an older rock performer (and an older women rocker at that) doesn't need to slack off because of age, but rather can continue bringing in the crowds to see what a great rock show is all about.

It's been forty years since the world first heard Tina's voice, but she has proved that the years don't have to make a difference to the voice that wants to sing — especially when it's a voice that so many still want to hear.

Studio Albums (as part of Ike and Tina Turner):
- THE SOUND OF IKE AND TINA TURNER (Sue, 1960)
- DON'T PLAY ME CHEAP (Sue, 1963)

- DYNAMITE (Sue, 1963)
- RIVER DEEP & MOUNTAIN HIGH (A&M, 1966)
- SO FINE (Special Music, 1968)
- OUTTA SEASON (Blue Thumb, 1969)
- HER MAN HIS WOMAN (Capitol, 1969)
- CUSSIN', CRYIN' AND CARRYIN' ON (Pompeii, 1969)
- WORKIN' TOGETHER (Liberty, 1970)
- SOMETHING'S GOT A HOLD OF ME (Harmony, 1971)
- FEEL GOOD (United Artists, 1972)
- NUTBUSH CITY LIMITS (United Artists, 1973)
- LET ME TOUCH YOUR MIND (United Artists, 1973)
- SWEET RHODE ISLAND RED (United Artists, 1974)
- TOO HOT TO HOLD (Charly, 1975)

Solo Selected Studio Albums:
- ACID QUEEN (Razor & Tie, 1975, reissued)
- ROUGH (United Artists, 1978)
- LOVE EXPLOSION (United Artists, 1979)
- PRIVATE DANCER (Capitol, 1984)
- BREAK EVERY RULE (Capitol, 1986)
- FOREIGN AFFAIR (Capitol, 1989)
- LOOK ME IN THE HEART (Alex, 1990)
- WILDEST DREAMS (Virgin, 1996)
- TWENTY FOUR SEVEN (EMI, 1999)

Best of the "Best Of" Albums:
- IKE AND TINA TURNER'S GREATEST HITS (United Artists, 1976)
- PROUD MARY: THE BEST OF IKE & TINA TURNER (EMI, 1991)
- SIMPLY THE BEST (Capitol, 1991)

Live Albums:
- IKE AND TINA TURNER IN PERSON (Minit, 1969)
- THE WORLD OF IKE AND TINA LIVE (United Artists, 1973)
- LIVE IN EUROPE (EMI, 1998)

~ 49 ~
Judie Tzuke

A couple of kids, some old folks, a man in a suit, the odd punk, wearers of denim and leather, some bikers, and throw in a couple of Goths for good measure — just a typical Judie Tzuke audience, really. And like her music, her fans cannot be branded or stereotyped. Radio stations are at a loss as to whether to play her records, not knowing if she was suitable for their program style. Meanwhile, several surveys have been conducted to determine the musical tastes of the 'typical' Judie Tzuke fan only to come to bizarre conclusions. Genesis and Marillion were a bit of a surprise; Kate Bush and Tori Amos were to be expected; but Black Sabbath and Alice Cooper?

It's this strange variety and the inability to brand that has been the downfall of Judie Tzuke throughout the years. At least to the thinking of the men in suits at the record companies. To her fans, however, Judie Tzuke is known for making excellent music, plain and simple.

Although some consider Judie to be a one-hit-wonder, that certainly is not the case. While her only hit single to date was the ballad *Stay With Me Till Dawn*, which entered the UK charts in the summer of 1979, her first seven albums, including her 1982 double live platter ROAD NOISE, were all top 40 hits in the UK. Unfortunately, while her sales were certainly adequate for a record label, trouble soon arose. A disagreement with Polydor records led to her seventh studio album, TURNING STONES, being withdrawn from sale as it entered the chart at number 57. Subsequently, the proposed tour also had to be cancelled and this led to the demise of Judie's chart success. It was another run-of-the-mill moment in Judie's career.

In the 20 years since Judie first hit the UK charts she has produced a most impressive back catalogue, managing to chock up eleven studio albums, three live albums, three "best of" compilations, twenty-three singles and two commercially released videos. All this with the assistance of no less than seven record companies. She even managed to take time off to produce two daughters and build her own recording studio.

Judie Myers was born at the Middlesex Hospital in London on April 3, 1956. Attending the School of Ballet and Drama in London's Piccadilly she was expelled on numerous occasions, but her father, Sefton Myers, known for his involvement in the production of JESUS CHRIST SUPERSTAR, managed to convince the school to take her back on each occasion. That was, of course, until his tragic death in 1971, where at the age of 15 Judie was expelled again. Only this time she didn't return.

It was also around this time that Judie decided to change her name back to that of her grandparents. The Tzuke's came to Britain in the 1920's and, in an attempt to "blend in," had changed their name to Myers, a popular name in Yorkshire at that time.

While schooling was not to her taste, Judie was interested in writing and begun writing poems at the age of 10. She started keeping a diary and at the bottom of each page she wrote a little poem. She also wrote poems to her history teacher, in an attempt to impress him. These poems got bigger as the years progressed. Eventually they changed into songs and at 15 she was performing in Folk clubs.

She knew she had talent and things might have been different if she had been a bit more prepared when, in 1973, she approached Rocket Records, a label just started by Elton John. Judie went for an audition and they were impressed with the two songs that she performed. Unfortunately these were the only two songs that she had and, when they asked her to return with some more of her compositions, she didn't dare go back.

So for several years Judie continued to perform in clubs and as a backing singer for a local band. Eventually she joined forces with Mike Paxman and formed the duo, Tzuke and Paxo. In 1977 they signed to the Good Earth record label and released a single called *These Are The Laws*. While with Good Earth Judie was introduced to another group, Omaha Sherriff, which contained two artistes who would later play a very important part in Judie's life. Bob Noble became a good friend of Judie's, co-writing and playing on numerous albums and tours. Paul Muggleton played, produced and later become Judie's partner and the father of her two children. It was also Paul who re-introduced Judie to Rocket Records in 1978. Female artists were very popular at the time so the duo with Mike was disbanded and Judie became the focal point.

Her first solo single, *For You*, was a beautiful ballad and an extremely risky release for an unknown. The single consisted of Judie performing several separate vocal tracks which were interwoven to form a magnificent ballad, almost completely a capella, with her only accompaniment being a classica string solo which some still refer to as a "lead break"! The single hovered around the outside of the charts and received substantial airplay but just didn't quite make it.

Stay With Me Till Dawn was another beautiful ballad which succeeded in proving Judie worthy of chart success, but it also sent out the message that she was strictly a ballad singer. This was definitely not the case; something that was clarified as the years progressed.

Judie stayed with Rocket Records for the release of her first three albums: WELCOME TO THE CRUISE, SPORTS CAR and I AM THE PHOENIX. Her popularity increased throughout the years, her albums were hits, her tours were sold out, and her singles were still released. All fine and good, but her name was quite oddly not appearing on the charts.

The reviews received for *Stay With Me Till Dawn* tended to point to a US audience. It was an opinion that the United States would love her music, but her one chance at becoming known in the US was foiled by more bad luck. Elton John was touring the US and had asked Judie to be his support, with the tour including a concert for over 450,000 in New York's Central Park. Her first album, WELCOME TO THE CRUISE was released in the US under the title of her UK hit single, *Stay With Me Till Dawn*. SPORTS CAR, her second album, was also released. It all sounded too good to be true, and it was.

Elton John's record distributor in the US, MCA, were somewhat disappointed at his decision to leave their label and, as a result, decided to drop all support for the tour and 'his' artists. This meant that Judie's albums were withdrawn from the US shelves and the tour had to proceed without record company backing. (Something that Judie was to become accustomed to over the years.) Judie was an unknown in the US and, since her records were unavailable, she received favorable reviews and gained a small following, but not much else.

Rocket as a small company was unable to promote Judie properly, so when the chance to join Chrysalis came along Judie took it. Chrysalis was a much larger record company and had successfully promoted artists such as Pat Benatar and Blondie over the years. Her first release with Chrysalis, SHOOT THE MOON, saw Judie making another slight change in direction. Her following had recently became very "rock oriented" and Judie was becoming a regular in the Heavy Metal press.

SHOOT THE MOON was another hit album and the tour to promote it was one of the biggest tours of any artist in the UK at that time, a grueling 46 dates including headlining the 1982 Glastonbury CND Festival. (This concert was filmed for television and is still circulating as an unofficial third live video.) The tour also

courtesy Hot Wacks

49 – Judie Tzuke

included two sold old dates at the former London Hammersmith Odeon. Glastonbury and the two Hammersmith dates were recorded and later released as a double live album, ROAD NOISE.

After one further album, RITMO, Judie parted company with Chrysalis. Although doing well on the charts in the UK, Chrysalis did not consider Judie to be one of their top acts. When it became clear that Chrysalis was not going to do much promotion for RITMO and had no intention of releasing the album in the US, Judie left. The following ten years saw the release of only four more studio albums — THE CAT IS OUT, TURNING STONES, LEFT HAND TALKING and WONDERLAND — for four separate record companies — Legacy, Polydor, Columbia and Essential Records. Judie wasn't idle in her personal life either. The bottom of her garden witnessed the erection of a large shed, later to become a recording studio, and Judie's first daughter, Bailey, was born. At the age of 12, Bailey can now be heard performing backing vocals on Judie's latest album.

Judie's second daughter, Tallula, was born in 1994 and Judie decided it was time to take another look at her life. She wasn't having much joy with record companies, large or small, so she decided to start her own record label, Big Moon Records. Her last two studio albums, UNDER THE ANGELS and SECRET AGENT, and one live album, OVER THE MOON, have been released on Big Moon.

Judie might not have been a major influence on many of the artists around today, but she's certainly well admired for her determination. Many an artist would have curled up and forgotten about the music scene, and it would have been incredibly easy for Judie to decide back in the mid-80's to quit. She was ahead of the game, well-known and popular. But Judie continued to write good music and, even after the disagreement with Polydor Records and the birth of Bailey, she still produced the goods, time after time.

She built her own recording studio, started her own record label and with the help of her long-time friend, Mike Paxman, the Judie Tzuke Web Site (www.tzuke.com) began. Judie continues to sell her records through this and her fan database built up over the years. Her tours are still large, although in smaller venues, and her records sell reasonably well. Rumors have hinted towards the release of a new single, her first in nearly eight years, and that a US distributor was interested in releasing her last two albums in the US as a sort of "Best of" compilation, but nothing appears to have taken place yet.

Meanwhile, Elton John, now back in command of Rocket Records, has recently returned the copyright of Judie's first three albums to her along with the master tapes. She has recently released all three through her own label and a tour, lovingly dubbed THE PHOENIX 2000 TOUR, is being undertaken to celebrate their release. The summer of 2000 should also witness a new album (DO YOU?), being recorded at present, and a subsequent promotional tour.

Stay With Me Till Dawn has again witnessed chart success having been released in the UK by a group called LUCID. The single received extensive radio airplay up until it's actual release but was then suddenly dropped from the radio play list. Even so, the single still managed to enter the top 40 but, without the backing of radio, was not able to survive long on the chart.

Judie is a very talented singer and songwriter with a lot to offer. Things have never gone smoothly for her, but hopefully, with the new developments in her career, things may improve. Her 1999 tour to promote her latest album, SECRET AGENT, witnessed a small group of fans pulling together to produce a tour program for her, her first in 14 years (these same fans have also pulled together to produce the PHOENIX 2000 tour program). Any artist that can influence their fans to such an extent deserves recognition for their achievements.

Selected Studio Albums:
- WELCOME TO THE CRUISE (Rocket Records, 1979; released as STAY WITH ME TIL DAWN in the US)
- SPORTSCAR (Rocket Records, 1980)
- I AM THE PHOENIX (Rocket Records, 1981)
- SHOOT THE MOON (Chrysalis Records, 1982)
- RITMO (Chrysalis Records, 1983)
- THE CAT IS OUT (Legacy, 1985)
- TURNING STONES (Polydor Records, 1989)
- LEFT HAND TALKING (Columbia Records, 1991)
- WONDERLAND (Essential Records, 1992)
- UNDER THE ANGELS (Big Moon Records, 1996)
- SECRET AGENT (Big Moon Records, 1998)
- DO YOU? (Big Moon Records, 2000)

Best of the "Best Of" Albums:
- THE BEST OF JUDIE TZUKE (Rocket Records, 1983)
- PORTFOLIO (Chrysalis Records, 1988)
- STAY WITH ME TILL DAWN (Spectrum Music Label, 1995)

Live Albums:
- ROAD NOISE - THE OFFICIAL BOOTLEG (Chrysalis Records, 1982)
- BBC - IN CONCERT (Windsong Records, 1995)
- OVER THE MOON (Big Moon Records, 1998)

~ 50 ~
Wendy O. Williams

Shocking. That seems to describe everything about Wendy. Shocking attitude, shocking music, shocking performances, shocking language, and certainly a shocking lack of clothes. She repulsed the public at large, yet still attracted their attention through outlandish stunts that bordered on the insane. And she did grab people's attention with her stunts, be it blowing up cars, chain-sawing guitars or just exposing herself on stage. In doing so, she knew that the payoff was in getting people's attention. After all, sometimes the best way to deliver a message is the most basic way — in your face.

Wendy was willing to take her character and push it to the limit. She really was the female equivalent of Alice Cooper, and it seemed just a little bit more shocking to have a woman do that type of thing on stage. If any of a number of male rock performers had taken a chain saw and cut a guitar in half, or blown up a television set, or even firebombed a car, we probably wouldn't have batted an eye, or even laughed at him. But here was a woman doing it, and it scared people.

courtesy Hot Wacks

Born May 28, 1949 in Webster, New York, there seems to be little public knowledge of her background. It seemed to be her preference that it remained that way as well. Instead, most biographies about Wendy start with her leaving home at 16 to see the world and ending up back in New York in 1974 working in live sex shows for promoter Rod Swenson in theaters all over 42nd Street. It was just about the time for the punk movement to begin in earnest, with the Ramones and several others in the New York area leading the way. Swenson, after filming music clips for the Ramones, Patti Smith and several others, saw the change in the wind and thought that there might be success waiting in the growing punk genre.

And understandably so. By 1978, everyone was hearing about the punk movement that was taking hold in the UK. As kids and parents in the early 1960's saw the Beatles spearhead the British Rock movement, many in the US saw (and feared) that the Sex Pistols were to lead the way for a second British invasion. The evening news and television shows were full of images of the punks, their bizarre hairstyles (especially the teased Mohawks), the safety pins through flesh, and the bodily fluids that seemed to be on display in concert footage. It was scary and/or exciting to a lot of people in the US, but there was one catch — it was happening in another country and not in the good ol' US of A. Even the Ramones found success easier in the UK and Europe than in the US. Everyone stateside was still getting out their boogie shoes or listening to gentle middle-of-the-road pop. There was no need to worry.

Swenson and Williams saw it was a prime opportunity to reach a spotlight in the US that had yet to be taken. Thus, on July 26, 1978, The Plasmatics debut at CBGB and the parents soon had to lock up not only their daughters, but their sons as well. Wendy slowly evolved into her character, with the Mohawk, the stripped-down wardrobe (sometimes with no top and usually only electrical tape covering her nipples) and a violent streak that sent shockwaves through the press and the public wherever she went. Along with her fellow band members — who helped with shocking images of their own (such as Richie Stotts with a Mohawk and wearing a little-girl's dress) — Wendy became an act to see just so people could claim that they'd survived a Plasmatics show. It didn't matter if they could play well or not, it was the show that mattered. In fact, it was two years before the band had a chance to record a full-length album (although several singles were released in the mean time).

1980 saw the release of the first Plasmatics album, NEW HOPE FOR THE WRETCHED, from Stiff Records and it was the breakthrough for the band whereby most of the US got a taste of Wendy for the first time. Soon, everyone was talking about The Plasmatics as the nastiest band on the planet, and even with the slow death of punk by the early 1980's (thanks to the new wave and Romantics movement), Wendy was becoming a household name in American.

Maybe a household name on the same level as the boogieman or Satan, but her name was becoming known just the same. Wendy wasn't only the lead singer, but the spokesperson for the band as well. Any chance she had to say or do something in front of the camera or the crowds, she was there. Whether anyone liked it or not.

1981 saw the release of two new albums from The Plasmatics, BEYOND THE VALLEY OF 1984 and METAL PRESTRESS. The band began appearing on television, mostly after hours, and Wendy began hitting the headlines for her outspoken language and attitude, and for the overtly sexual content of the shows. In fact, by the end of 1981, Wendy began having trouble in certain cities when the band played and faced obscenities charges in Cleveland and Milwaukee. Still, it was the shock that mattered.

Wendy began 1982 working with Lemmy of Mötörhead on a remake of the classic Tammy Wynette song, *Stand By Your Man*. It was followed up with the album COUP d'ETAT, which had the band filming one of the most outrageous music videos ever for *The Damned*. The video involved Wendy standing on top of an out-of-control school bus containing dynamite as it raced toward a wall of television sets in the desert. During this, Wendy sings the track only to jump off right before the bus hits the wall and explodes. In typical Wendy fashion, she ended the song looking at the wreckage in boredom and dusting herself off as she walked away.

The band was well-known, but that popularity didn't translate into huge record sales or concerts around the country. By 1983, The Plasmatics had gone through personnel changes and it was clear that Wendy was becoming the sole center of the group. It was during this year that The Plasmatics opened for KISS on their CREATURES OF THE NIGHT tour. Gene Simmons of KISS noticed the reaction Wendy got on stage and decided to produce Wendy's first solo album, the excellent WOW, released in 1984 by Passport Records. It was to be one of the highlights of her career, with Wendy doing another outstanding stunt in a music video — grabbing hold of a rope-ladder suspended from a helicopter just as the car she was driving goes over a cliff. In making the album, Wendy ended up making a clear transition from the world of punk to the new emerging world of heavy metal. As with punk, she became the leading American spokeswoman for the genre and there was nothing anyone would dare say against it.

Wendy followed up that album with another called KOMMANDER OF KAOS in 1986, while the same year saw her in the great parody film, REFORM SCHOOL GIRLS (whose soundtrack albums has four songs performed by Wendy). The film appearance, although not her first (CANDY GOES TO HOLLYWOOD is normally listed as her first in 1979, a film that showed Wendy's unique talent with ping-pong balls), would lead to several other television and film appearances over the next few years, along with some theatrical appearances as Magenta in a St. Louis production of THE ROCKY HORROR SHOW in 1987.

courtesy Hot Wacks

By 1991, however, Wendy had shocked her fans once again. Sick of the business side of show business, and with the lack of success that came with her rap album in 1988 (Ultrafly And The Hometown Girls' DEFFEST AND BADDEST), Wendy moved with Swenson to Storrs, Connecticut and began working as a wildlife animal rehabilitator and in a health food co-op. It was there that Wendy quietly spent the next seven years of her life until April 6, 1998 when she committed suicide in a wooded area near her home.

To many it was a surprise to hear that a woman who seemed to want to live life to its fullest would end her own life. Yet, Wendy saw it as a matter of control, just as she saw the rest of her life as a series of cases where she had to become the leader and take charge. Most of us disagree with her reasoning. But, then again, her actions allowed her to do something that she hadn't done in years — she shocked us all once again.

Selected Studio Albums (as part of the Plasmatics):
- ◦ NEW HOPE FOR THE WRETCHED (Stiff, 1980)
- ◦ BEYOND THE VALLEY OF 1984 (Stiff, 1981)
- ◦ METAL PRIESTESS (Stiff, 1981)
- ◦ COUP D'ETAT (Capitol 1982)
- ◦ MAGGOTS (WOW/Sledgehammer/Profile Records, 1987)

Studio Album (as part of Ultrafly and the Hometown Girls):
- ◦ DEFFEST AND BADDEST (Profile/Sledgehammer, 1988)

Selected Studio Albums:
- ◦ WOW (Passport Records, 1984)
- ◦ KOMMANDER OF KAOS (Gigasaurus/Sledgehammer, 1986)

Live Albums:
- ◦ FUCK 'N ROLL (Jackhammer Records, 1985)

Appendix A
~ What About The Bands? ~

The focus of this book has been looking at women in rock music and pointing out the outstanding solo artists who influenced other performers over the years. Still, it's hard to list just a handful of performers, knowing full well that in doing so we ends up ignoring so many others. Not only are there women who have been in bands that have left a mark on the rock music genre overall, but there are certainly a good number of bands that were unique because they did not have any men in them. In a genre that is so male-based, and one where women rockers are constantly teased as being merely the front for the "guys who are actually playing the music," there must be room in a book like this to mention some of the bands made up entirely of women. The only regret is that there is not enough room to mention more. If anything, however, the groups listed below are just the tip of the iceberg when it comes to bands that proved you didn't need to be a man to play great music, you just had to have guts.

A1: The Bangles

If some felt that The Go-Go's were unfairly treated with respect to their musical talents, then the general attitude about The Bangles borders on the criminal. A band born out of an underground movement in California based on a Psychedelic sound, they went

through numerous name changes before settling on The Bangles. Because the band was made up of not only talented women, but attractive women as well, the critical response to the band's music ranged from assumptions of studio musicians playing everything to not being progressive for the women's movement. That still didn't stop them from having several Top Ten hits and becoming one of the most successful rock acts of the 1980's. Still, the "pretty girls" stigma helped lead to the demise of the band and they broke up in 1989.

Recommended Albums:
- ETERNAL FLAME: BEST OF THE BANGLES
- ALL OVER THE PLACE
- EVERYTHING

A2: The Donnas

If a scientific experiment had genetically joined The Runaways with The Ramones, The Donnas would have been the results. A blistering punk Rock and Roll sound based around a group of young women who use a variation of The Ramones' name ranking (i.e. instead of the last name being changed, every member of The  Donnas goes by the first name of Donna). Of course, the names are just cosmetic, but it's still a great homage to the past. Originally called Raggedy Anne, then The Electrocutes, The Donnas are fulfilling the promises that earlier all-female bands from the early 1990's never quite fulfilled.

Recommended Albums:
- DONNAS
- AMERICAN TEENAGE ROCK & ROLL MACHINE
- GET SKINTIGHT

A3: Fanny

An out-and-out Rock and Roll all-female band that started about four years too soon, Fanny got together in 1970, made up of Nicky Barclay on keyboards, June Millington on guitar, Jean Millington on bass and Alice de Buhr on drums. The band found some success in Europe in their early days and was quite successful in the club scene, but it didn't translate into record sales. By 1974 they had released their final album (and their only one through the then-new label, Casablanca) and broke up. Ironically, their last album featured Patti Quatro, the sister of Suzi who found mega-success the same year that Fanny broke up. The Runaways also started within a year of Fanny's demise and found more success as well.

Band members also appeared on two Barbra Streisand albums, while Nickey Barclay went on to perform with Joe Cocker on his MAD DOGS AND ENGLISHMEN tour and album. For anyone wanting an early dose of what was to come with Suzi, The Runaways and several of the other acts of the 1970's, give Fanny a spin.

Recommended Albums:
- RAINNY
- SHARITY BALL
- ROCK 'N' ROLL SURVIVORS

A4: Girlschool

courtesy Hot Wacks

Typically lumped in with the punk bands of the late 1970's (mainly because they were an all-female band and writers were too lazy to disassociate them from the all-female punk bands of the era), Girlschool was one of the first all-female heavy metal bands to find success in the 1980's. An excellent band (helped out in their early days by Mötörhead), Girlschool never quite reached the level of success that was due them. Highly recommended to anyone interested in the heavy metal movement of the 1980's.

Although the band broke up in 1988 after many member changes, three original members — Kim McAuliffe, Denise Dufort and Kelly Johnson — reformed the band in 1992.

Recommended Albums:
- DEMOLITION
- HIT & RUN
- PLAY DIRTY
- TAKE A BITE

A5: The Go-Go's

This is a band created, destroyed and recreated by its reputation. Starting out as The Misfits in 1978, they became known in the California area for their music, which was a

courtesy Hot Wacks

mixture of punk and dance (although mostly punk in their early days). The Go-Go's became successful first in the UK and then in the US, but by the time of their first album, BEAUTY AND THE BEAT, was released, a lot of the punk-edge of the band had disappeared, replaced by a new-wavish aura of dance Rock and Roll. Because they refused to fit the genre properly, their earlier fans soon felt that the band was betraying their punk roots (or saying that they never had them in the first place and were only posers), while others simply wrote them off as fluff.

The Go-Go's came back with VACATION in 1982 and TALK SHOW in 1984, but broke up by 1985 thanks to a combination of drugs, bad feelings and slow sales. Belinda Carlisle, the lead singer, and Janet Wiedlin (guitar) launched solo careers, while other members continued to work in music in other capacities. The band is still viewed as the quintessential all-female new-wave band and many people still remember their hits. The Go-Go's reformed in 1995 and released the album GOOD GIRL.

Recommended Albums:
- BEAUTY AND THE BEAT
- RETURN TO THE VALLEY OF THE GO-GO'S

A6: L7

Formed in 1985 in Los Angeles, L7 is a group born more out of the punk movement than the grunge movement that they typically get lumped into. Not overtly pursuing a political agenda as were many of the genre's bands between the late 1980's and early 1990's, L7's music typically is and remains more in the style of punk and hard-rock. For a time it looked like they was ready to break through into a type of superstar status that came to bands such as Smashing Pumpkins and Nirvana, but it never occurred. The band can also be seen performing briefly in John Waters' movie, SERIAL MOM, as the band Camel Lips.

Recommended Albums:
- L7
- BRICKS ARE HEAVY
- THE BEAUTY PROCESS
- SLAP-HAPPY

A7: The Raincoats

Formed as a self-confessed "art school" band with no musical background, The Raincoats became one of the best remembered of the women groups from the short-lived punk scene. Beginning with Palmolive (who had just left The Slits) on drums, the original lineup also included Ana Da Silva on guitar, Gina Birch on bass and Vicky Aspinall on guitar and violin. The band went through numerous changes over the years and broke up in 1984, but had a resurgence in the early 1990's after both Kurt Cobain and Kim Gordon wrote liner notes for the reissues of their first three studio albums. Sometimes referred to as the "godmothers of grunge," the core personnel of the band, Ana Da Silva and Gina Birch, reformed The Raincoats in 1994 and have released a couple of albums since that time.

Recommended Albums:
- THE RAINCOATS
- ODYSHAPE
- MOVING
- LOOKING IN THE SHADOWS

A8: Rock Goddess

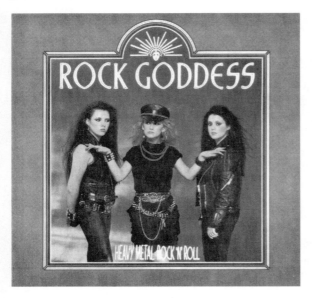

Although around for nearly eight years, this British trio only made two albums and both of them were released in 1983. Still, Rock Goddess was one of the few examples of an all-female heavy metal band, and typically the only one that could be seen in the magazines besides Girlschool. Their version of Gary Glitter's *Didn't Know I Loved You* is a killer example of the early 1980's metal scene. Both albums were reissued in 1998 by Renaissance and are definitely worth a listen.

Recommended Albums:
  ○ ROCK GODDESS
  ○ HELL HATH NO FURY

A9: The Runaways

Initially formed by Joan Jett, The Runaways were reinvented by musician / producer Kim Fowley as a group response to the success of Suzi Quatro in Europe. For this reason alone, the band is consistently looked upon as a manufactured image, much like The Monkees in the 1960's. And, just like The Monkees, the group was made up of individual musicians that actually put a lot of time and energy into performing a lot of great out-and-out rock music. The punk and heavy metal influence of later women performers had roots in The Runaways, no matter how much some would deny it. This was the starting place not only for Joan Jett and Lita Ford (who have their own solo entries in this book), but also Cherrie Currie. Currie recorded two excellent albums after The Runaways (BEAUTY'S ONLY SKIN DEEP and MESSIN' WITH THE BOYS), and should be a much bigger name than she is today.

Recommended Albums:
- THE RUNAWAYS
- QUEENS OF NOISE
- Cherrie's BEAUTY'S ONLY SKIN DEEP
- and check out the Jett and Ford entries for their solo albums

A10: The Slits

One of the first well-known all-female punk bands, The Slits are a perfect representation of what good did come out of the punk movement. Composed of musicians who didn't know how to play their instruments (much like The Raincoats, created a year afterwards), The Slits eventually grew into their roles and adapted a unique style to their music. The original all-female line-up of the group was compromised in 1978 after Palmolive left to join The Raincoats and Budgie joined to replace her on drums. (Budgie later joined Siouxsie Sioux in her band. See her main entry for more details.) Bruce Smith later replaced Budgie in 1979. And true to form for the punk movement, the band broke up relatively early in its career and by 1981 the band members were all off doing work with other bands.

Notorious for posing topless on the cover of their first album (which some viewed as pandering to the very same sexual stereotype that it was trying to lampoon), The Slits are remembered today as an ancestor to the whole "riot grrrl" phenomena. The band certainly was experimental, and while some of their early work is hard to listen to, the later material certainly has a lot of bite.

Recommended Albums:
- CUT
- RETURN OF THE GIANT SLITS
- RESTROSPECTIVE

Appendix B
~ The Girl Groups ~

Rock and Roll music wasn't the beginning of the girl-groups. There were certainly vocal groups that were very well-known in the pop charts long before Rock and Roll came along. We need only look at the prosperous career of the Andrews Sisters to see how successful the girl-groups of the 1940's were (with movie roles as well as radio shows being just some of the benefits heaped on them based on their recording work).

Girl-groups as a term, however, typically is used to describe the group of women who were singing (normally in trios) some of the biggest Rock and Roll hits of the 1960's. It was also a genre that ran out of gas by the end of the 1960's as fans more and more began to expect performers to be playing instruments and writing their own material as well as singing. Still, the genre has not died out completely, and there are examples of vocal groups having rock hits after the girl-group era was over.

Either way, thanks to the girl-groups, many major Rock and Roll hits made it to the fans over the years. It was also the birthplace of stardom for many women performers who would eventually break away and become well-known solo artists.

B1: The Angels

Best remembered for their hit, *My Boyfriend's Back*, in 1963, The Angels found that song to be the high point of their chart career, although they had a few other hits during the 1960's, including *'Till*, *Cry Baby Cry* and *I Adore Him*. The group was originally made up of Barbara Allibut, her sister Phyllis Allibut and Linda Jansen and was formed in 1961. In 1962, Jansen left to be replaced by Peggy Santiglia and it is her voice that can be heard on *My Boyfriend's Back*. The group continued throughout most of the 1960's, but they never again quite hit the heights of their 1963 single.

Recommended Albums:
  ◦ MY BOYFRIEND'S BACK
  ◦ THE BEST OF THE ANGELS

B2: Bananarama

An example of a latter-day girl-group that found success in an era where you would have thought it impossible. Bananarama came out of the new wave / romantics era of British music as a backlash against the punk movement that was already ebbing in the UK, and at first featured a lighthearted variety of music in the early 1980's. This changed with their 1984 single, *Robert DeNiro's Waiting*, which dealt with rape, and the group tried to move towards more serious themes after that. They had a huge hit with a cover of Shocking Blue's song, *Venus*, in

1986, but in 1987 Siobhan Fahey departed (and later become part of Shakespeare's Sister), leaving Keren Woodward and Sarah Dallin to continue the group with Jacquie O'Sullivan. O'Sullivan left in 1991 and Woodward and Dallin continued as a duo for two more albums.

Recommended Albums:
- DEEP SEA SKIVING
- BANANARAMA
- TRUE CONFESSIONS
- GREATEST HITS COLLECTION

B3: The Chantels

The Chantels were one of the first girl-groups to become known for a Rock and Roll hit, recording the single *Maybe* in 1957. Started in 1956 with Arlene Smith, Lois Harris, Sonia Goring, Jackie Landry and Rene Minus, Smith was the designated leader of the group and she also wrote most of their early material (including *Maybe*). The band had a few more hits before and after the 1958 success of *Maybe*, but Smith left in 1959, and was followed soon after by Lois Harris. The band continued until 1970, when they broke up. Smith has since reformed the band with four

other women and has performed with them off and on over the years.

Recommended Albums:
- ○ THE BEST OF THE CHANTELS

B4: The Chiffons

An early New York girl-group from the 1960's, The Chiffons' biggest hit was *He's So Fine*, with *One Fine Day* being remembered just as easily by fans of the era. The band was also known as The Four Pennies. They formed in the Bronx during 1960, but 1963 was the peak of their success and they broke up by the beginning of the 1970's.

Recommended Albums:
- ○ ONE FINE DAY
- ○ GREATEST HITS

B5: The Chordettes

Formed in 1946, The Chordettes first big hit was *Mr. Sandman* in 1954 (an early pop hit that resulted in more girl-group material aimed at the doo-wop and Rock and Roll

markets). The group, being made up of white girls, was typically used to cash in on R&B hits that would never have made it on the pop charts in the 1950's without first being "whitened" for safety. They had a lot of hits because of this and helped the crossover occur that led to the whole Rock and Roll phenomena. They broke up in 1961 after the released of their final hit, *Never on Sunday*.

Recommended Albums:
- ○ THE BEST OF THE CHORDETTES

B6: The Crystals

Formed in 1961 in Brooklyn, New York, The Crystals were Barbara Alston, Lala Brooks, Dee Dee Kennibrew, Mary Thomas and Patricia Wright. They were one of the best known of the girl-groups that worked with Phil Spector and they have a variety of hits, although two of them (*He's a Rebel* and *He's Sure the Boy I Love*) were actually recorded by Darlene Love and The Blossoms. Their other hits included *Da Doo Ron Ron* and *Then He Kissed Me*. The group lost momentum after 1965 when Patricia Wright left and they broke away from Spector. Frances Collins joined the group to replace Wright, but they never built steam again and officially broke up in 1966. The group reformed in 1971 and there have been several versions of The Crystals performing since then, but only Kennibrew still is involved in any version of the group today.

Recommended Albums:
- o HE'S A REBEL
- o THE GREATEST HITS
- o THE BEST OF THE CRYSTALS

B7: Labelle

If KISS was the demented 1970's version of the pop-band, and Parliament-Funkadelic was the demented 1970's version of the soul-group, then Labelle was the demented 1970's version of the girl-group. In fact, they originally were a girl-group — formed in 1962 as The Blue Belles. Encountering the end of the road for girl-groups by the beginning of the 1970's, they were reborn as Labelle and

began dressing in futuristic outfits and singing incredible rock-fused R&B songs that ran up the charts. They broke up in 1977, leaving us with the outstanding solo careers of Patti LaBelle, Sarah Dash and Nona Hendryx, but they proved beyond a doubt that the girls could be just as outrageous as the boys during the 1970's.

Recommended Albums:
- o PRESSUR COOKIN'
- o NIGHTBIRDS
- o LADY MARMALADE: THE BEST OF PATTI AND LABELLE

B8: Martha & The Vandellas

Along with The Supremes, Martha & The Vandellas are remembered as the best of the girl-groups to come out of Motown. The group began in 1963 when singer Mary Wells didn't show up for a contractually-obligated recording session on a new Motown single. Having known Reeves as a singer from her previous work on a single with her group The Del-Phis back in 1960 (which was released under the name of The Vels), and knowing that she was in the company's secretarial pool, the producer had Reeves brought in to record the single. The record, *I'll Have to Let Him Go*, became the first release for Martha & The Vandellas. The group went through several changes over time, but Reeves was a constant and they had many hits, including *Dancing in the Streets*, *Heatwave*, *Nowhere to Run* and *Quicksand*. The group broke up in 1972, and Martha Reeves began a solo career after suing Motown to get out of her contract. She would eventually win a suit against Motown in 1989 for back royalties (one of the first artists of the period to do so) and has occasionally done Vandellas team-ups since then while also continuing her solo career.

Recommended Albums:
- HEATWAVE
- DANCE PARTY
- DANCING IN THE STREET: THEIR GREATEST HITS

B9: The Shangri-Las

If girl-groups are best remembered for singing songs that told heartbreaking stories of lost loves and ruined lives, The Shangri-Las were a major reason for it. Best remembered for *Leader of the Pack*, The Shangri-Las were formed in 1963 with Marge and Mary Ann Ganser (identical twins) and Mary and Betty Weiss. Produced by George "Shadow" Morton, their first single was *Remember (Walkin' in the Sand)* and the hits just kept on coming after that. The group eventually broke up in 1969 and is one of the few groups that haven't reunited as have many of the girl-groups over the years.

Recommended Albums:
- THE BEST OF THE SHANGRI-LAS

B10: The Shirelles

One of the longest lasting of the early 1960's girl-groups, The Shirelles helped define the "girl-groups sound" of the period with their hits *Will You Love Me Tomorrow*, *Soldier Boy* and *Dedicated to the One I Love*. The group never had another Top 40 hit after 1963, but they continued to work together until the 1970's as a unit, doing more soul-oriented music as time went on.

Recommended Albums:
- ANTHOLOGY (1959-1964)
- 25 ALL-TIME GREATEST HITS

B11: The Supremes

The Supremes are typically not thought of in the same terms as the other girl-groups listed here, particularly because of Diana Ross' success after she left the group in early 1970. Formed in 1961 in Detroit, Michigan, The Supremes were Diana Ross, Mary Wilson and Florence Ballard. They were taken under Barry Gordy's wing at Motown and became one of the most popular groups (girl-group or otherwise) of the 1960's. Their hits included *Stop! In the Name of Love*, *Baby Love*, *Come See About Me*, *You Keep Me Hangin' On*, and several others, and would proved to be a true crossover from the R&B charts to the pop charts. Ballard left the band in 1967, and was replaced by Cindy Birdsong,

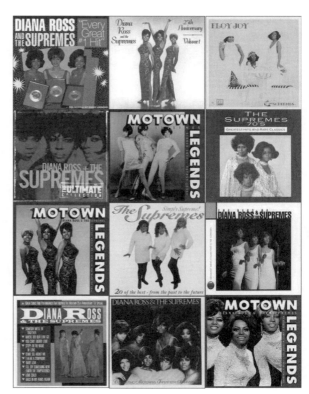

and the group then became Diana Ross and The Supremes. After Ross left in 1970, Jean Terrell replaced her and the Supremes continued until 1977. Commonly forgotten is the fact that The Supremes still had hits after Diana Ross left, but with Ross becoming a pop superstar (although rarely rocking like she did in her early days), The Supremes became little more than a footnote in her history.

Recommended Albums:
- WHERE DID OUR LOVE GO?
- LIVE AT THE APOLLO
- LOVE CHILD
- ANTHOLOGY
- THE ULTIMATE COLLECTION

Appendix C
~ In The Spotlight ~

As seen already, there are many big-name women solo artists, girl-groups and all-female bands that have made their mark in rock music. But there's still more. Many bands have come and gone that have featured women as part of the group, and several of them have also left their mark on the musical genre. Some are readily thought of as an intricate member of the band (would it be The Talking Heads without Tina Weymouth, or X without Exene Cervenka?), while others have been the focus of the group (after all, the band wasn't called The Waves, they were called Katrina And The Waves). Either way, these women have had their careers shaped by the bands that they were in and not mentioning some of them would be ignoring a whole other segment of women in rock.

C1: Christina Amphlett

courtesy KAOS2000

Why The Divinyls are not more well-known is almost impossible to understand. Many people would probably know them from their 1991 hit *I Touch Myself*, but they had been around since 1981 and recording albums since their first EP in 1982. Based out of Sydney, Australia, Amphlett provides the lusty vocals for this band that has always been produced wickedly hard-rock style music with lyrics that border on seduction. Dressed up in a schoolgirl's outfit (like a counterpart to Angus Young in AC/DC, another Australian band), Amphlett brought a lot of the lyrics to life and she certainly perfected the pouting lips. Excellent band, although only Amphlett and Mark McEntee remain of the original lineup. Highly recommended material.

Recommended Albums:
- ○ DESPERATE
- ○ WHAT A LIFE!
- ○ DIVINYLS
- ○ MAKE YOU HAPPY (1981-1993) (best of)

C2: Dale Bozzio

Dale was the lead singer of the early 1980's band, Missing Persons. Created by Dale with her husband, former Frank Zappa drummer Terry Bozzio (and also considered one of the best rock drummers in the business), the band worked with a new wave sound built on keyboard and synth-drums. Their videos for *Word* and *Destination Unknown* were a staple of early MTV broadcasting back in 1982-83 and it wasn't unusual to turn on MTV in those early days and see Dale in her clear plastic, space-age outfit. Dale's vocals were also quite unique with her frequent hiccups and haulty style. The band broke up in 1986, along with the marriage between Dale and Terry. Dale went on to record one solo album in 1988, but there have been no more records since that time.

Recommended Albums:
- RIOT IN ENGLISH (solo album)
- SPRING SESSION M
- RHYME & REASON

C3: Exene Cervenka

One of the first popular punk bands to come out of California was X, and Exene Cervenka was not only their lead singer, but one of their best writers as well. The band became known for their experimentation (at a time when most punk bands were either already gone or retreading themselves into non-existence). Unfortunately, their persistence in attempting new angles with their music left them with more of a cult following and they've recorded only sporadically since the early 1990's. Exene (who also goes by the last name of Cervenkova) has recorded a few solo albums over the years, which are somewhat more folk-rock oriented than the X material. She has also been involved with poetry publications and has worked with Lydia Lunch.

Recommended Albums:
- LOS ANGELES
- UNDER THE BIG BLACK SUN
- MORE FUN IN THE NEW WORLD
- UNCLOGGED (live)
- OLD WIVES' TALES (solo)
- RUNNING SACRED (solo)

C4: Martha Davis

In 1982 it seemed that The Motels could do no wrong. They were certainly doing well in the charts thanks to *Only the Lonely* (and *Take the L* was a big hit as well). Martha Davis was the lead singer of the band when they formed in 1973, featuring her deep vocals wrapped around a variety of songs dealing with the inner turmoil of love. The band recorded two albums before their 1982 release, ALL 4 ONE, and continued their hit-making with their follow-up album in 1983, LITTLE ROBBERS (which included the single, *Suddenly Last Summer*). Unfortunately, The Motels began repeating itself with new material and after the failure of their next albums they broke up in 1987. At their heights in 1982, Davis was often put into the same category of strong female vocalists as Pat Benatar, Stevie Nicks and many others. If the band had continued with its success, Davis would probably still be put in the same category today.

Recommended Albums:
- ALL 4 ONE
- LITTLE ROBBERS
- NO VACANCY (best of)

C5: Katrina Leskanich

Born in Topeka, Kansas, Katrina arrived in England in the mid-1970's when her father's Air Force work caused the family to move there. By the early 1980's she had joined forces with three musicians (including Kimberly Rew, formerly of Soft Boy) and begun playing shows as The Waves. Sometimes compared to Chrissie Hyndes, Katrina had a hit single with the band in 1983 with *Walking on Sunshine*. The band continued with an energetic mixture of charming pop and clear guitar melodies for a few years (sounding more like a positive and upbeat Joan Jett And The Blackhearts than anything else), but they never again quite hit the heights of 1983. After an attempt at heavy metal in 1989, the band broke up only to reform in 1997. They won the 1997 Eurovision Song Contest with *Love Shine a Light* and released one more album before Katrina left the band for good. 1998 and 1999 saw Katrina doing her own radio show on BBC Radio 2, and currently she's working on recording and touring with her first solo album. By the way, *Do You Want Crying?* is a killer power-pop song.

Recommended Albums:
- WALKING ON SUNSHINE
- KATRINA & THE WAVES
- ANTHOLOGY (best of)

C6: Annabella Lwin

Born October 31, 1965, Annabella was a provocative choice to join the band Bow Wow Wow after original singer Boy George left. The group had originally been put together by Malcolm McLaren, manager of The Sex Pistols, and was made up of three members of the original Adam And The Ants (Matthew Ashman, Leigh Gorman and David Barbarossa). Annabella had a great voice, striking beauty (although best remembered for her Mohawk hairstyle), and was only 14 at the time. The group played music with a strong African beat to it and had a hit with a cover of *I Want Candy* in 1982. Annabella left the group in 1983 for a solo career (her biggest single was a cover of *Fever*), but rejoined the band in 1998 for another album. Well worth a listen, especially for fans of Adam Ant's music.

Recommended Albums:
- I WANT CANDY
- THE BEST OF BOW WOW WOW

C7: Shirley Manson

Garbage was a band built around the musical talents of three producers, Butch Vig, Duke Erikson and Steve Marker. Although originally playing only as a jam sessions, the three eventually decided to recruit a vocalist for recordings and shows. Manson had already worked with two bands, Goodbye Mr. MacKenzie and Angelfish (which released an album in 1994 featuring Manson) before joining Garbage. The band became quite successful after the release of the first album in 1995, and followed it up with another album in 1998. Since the band is strictly a side-project for for the three producers, they have only worked on material when time permits.

Recommended Albums:
- GARBAGE
- VERSION 2.0
- and Angelfish's ANGELFISH

C8: Christine McVie

Always remembered as being part of Fleetwood Mac, her solo career has often been overshadowed by those of other Mac members like Stevie Nicks, Lindsey Buckingham and even Mick Fleetwood. McVie had worked as a singer with the Spencer Davis group in the 1960's and also worked with the short-lived Chicken Shack before recording a solo album in 1970. After marrying John McVie of Fleetwood Mac, Christine began singing and playing keyboards for the band and went on to write many of their biggest hits of the 1970's and 80's. She also had a hit album with her second solo record in 1984, CHRISTINE MCVIE.

courtesy Hot Wacks

Recommended Albums:
- CHRISTINE PERFECT (first solo album)
- CHRISTINE MCVIE (1984 solo album)
- Fleetwood Mac's RUMOURS
- Chicken Shack's FORTY BLUE FINGERS
- FRESHLY PACKED

C9: Kate Pierson & Cindy Wilson

courtesy Hot Wacks

Without these two, how would The B-52's ever have come up with their name? The name of the band was based on Southern slang for the large bouffant hairstyles worn by Kate and Cindy and was just a small example of their continuous party feel. Sometimes dismissed as retro, and sometimes as just a dance band, The B-52's were formed by Kate, Cindy, Fred Schneider, Ricky Wilson and Keith Strickland in 1976 as more of a lark than a seriousness undertaking. It was that sense of fun that has always stuck with them, even at times of great stress, like of the passing of Ricky Wilson in 1985. The B-52's found their greatest success with the release of their album COSMIC THING, which included the hits *Love Shack* and *Roam*. Cindy left the band in 1990, but returned in 1998 for their greatest hits collection tour. An obvious example that humor does belong in rock music and that women can deliver it just as well as any man can.

Recommended Albums:
- ○ WILD PLANET
- ○ COSMIC THING
- ○ GOOD STUFF
- ○ TIME CAPSULE (best of)

C10: Gwen Stefani

Gwen was the lead singer of No Doubt, which burst onto the alternative rock scene in 1995 with their album TRAGIC KINGDOM. Gwen formed the band in 1987, along with

the ska band Madness, with Eric Stefani, John Spence and Tony Kanai. After Spence passed away in 1987, Tom Dumont and Adrian Young joined them. After signing with Interscope in 1992, their first album, NO DOUBT, was released in 1992. A mixture of ska and new wave, it did nothing on the charts. In response, Eric Stefani left the band and they moved towards more cutting-edge musical styles. No Doubt released a new album in 2000, RETURN OF SATURN.

Recommended Albums:
- NO DOUBT
- TRAGIC KINGDOM
- RETURN OF SATURN

C11: Kirsty Wallace

Kirsty is probably better known as Poison Ivy Rorschach to any fan of The Cramps, a band she started with Lux Interior (a.k.a. Erick Purkhiser) in 1976. Their combined loves for the rockabilly music of the 1950's, the bizarre, and certain "white trash" elements of American culture resulted in what can only be described as the funniest band to ever come out of the 1970's punk revolution. A

great driving rock beat mixed with Lux's monotone vocals made this a great band to listen to in the middle of the night. Although other members have come and gone, Ivy and Lux still continue with The Cramps. Ivy produced the excellent STAY SICK! album in 1990.

Recommended Albums:
- GRAVEST HITS
- SMELL OF FEMALE
- DATE WITH ELVIS
- STAY SICK!

C12: Tina Weymouth

Weymouth's involvement in The Talking Heads is enough to get a mention here, with their quirky style of rock music, sliced by keyboards and off-centered lyrics. The Talking Heads started in the early 1970's with David Byrne and Chris Frantz. Jerry Harrison joined in 1976. They produced a lot of material that attracted fans and tremendous critical praise over the years. Weymouth also worked with Frantz on a side-project, The Tom Tom Club, which had a Top 40 hit in 1981 with *Genius of Love*. Both bands went on simultaneously for several years, although The Talking Heads broke up in 1991 (with

Frantz, Harrison and Weymouth teaming up in 1996 as The Heads) and The Tom Tom Club has not released an album since 1992.

Recommended Albums:
- ◦ TOM TOM CLUB
- ◦ STOP MAKING SENSE
- ◦ FEAR OF MUSIC

C13: Ann & Nancy Wilson

If these two artists had been solo performers they no doubt would have made it into the Top 50 of this book. But their place is really with their band, Heart. The sisters became interested in music at an early age, with Nancy taking up guitar and flute, while Ann learn a variety of instruments. Nancy later became a folksinger, while Ann joined an all-male vocal group called Heart in 1973. Nancy joined Heart in 1974 and the band became well-known in the Vancouver area. They recorded their first album, DREAMBOAT ANNIE, in 1975 and when it sold quickly in Canada, CBS picked up Heart in 1977. Although the band was started before the Wilson sisters joined, they became the focus and survivors of the band over the years, going through some slumps and then another huge leap in popularity with their 1985 self-titled album. Their popularity has ebbed since then, but the two continue to work together and even formed an acoustic group in the early 1990's called The Lovemongers during a hiatus in Heart. Through it all, they've been the backbone of one of the few bands from the 1970's who haven't either broken up or called simply it quits, continuing to make new music to the present day.

Recommended Albums:
- ◦ DREAMBOAT ANNIE
- ◦ LITTLE QUEEN
- ◦ DOG & BUTTERFLY
- ◦ BEBE LE STRANGE
- ◦ HEART
- ◦ BAD ANIMALS THE ROAD HOME
- ◦ GREATEST HITS

~ Recommended Reading ~

As mentioned in the Introduction to this book, there have been a few books about women in rock music published over the years. There are not, perhaps, as many as one would hope, nor are they always worth the time to bother reading. Unfortunately, some of the best ones are either limited-run publications or now out of print. Of the books still out there, however, here are a few that are worth searching for:

- SIRENS OF SONG by Aida Pavletich. Published 1980 by Da Capo Press, New York, NY. ISBN 0-036-80162-0
- SHE BOP by Lucy O'Brien. Published 1995 by Penguin Books, New York, NY. ISBN 0 14 02.5155 3
- WOMEN ON TOP by James Dickerson. Published by Billboard Books, New York, NY. ISBN 0-8230-8489-2
- SHE'S A REBEL by Gillian G. Gaar. Published 1992 by Seal Press, Seattle, WA. ISBN 1-878067-08-7

Several autobiographies have been printed over the past decades from a variety of the artists listed in this book, and many are still available in stores. Again, some are better than others, but a quick look through the local library will probably turn up several. I would also recommend Chip Deffaa's book, BLUE RHYTHMS (published in 1996 by University of Illinois Press, Chicago, IL. ISBN 0-252-02203-3) for excellent reporting of the Blues and an excellent summary of LaVern Baker.

Of course, there is also the Internet. Many of the artists listed already have their own official web sites, as well as appearing on sites connected to their current and former labels, so a good search-engine should help track down information easily. There are two web sites in particular that I would like to mention because of their easy access to additional information that may interest readers of this book:

- WOMEN IN ROCK
  (http://www.bluemoon.net/~sumosen)
  is simply a list of links which will take the user directly to official or fan-based sites for a variety of women in music. It's well worth a look and was a tremendous help during the research for this book.

- ROCKIN' RINA'S PUNK WOMEN IN THE 1970'S
  (http://www.comnet.ca/~rina/index.html)
  is an excellent site full of information pertaining to exactly what its title says — info on women punk rockers of the 1970's. Great work on the site and enough information to be a candidate itself for publication.

COLLECT THE WHOLE SET

Psychedelia	ISBN 1-896522-40-8	Pop	ISBN 1-896522-25-4
Alternative Rock	ISBN 1-896522-19-X	Punk	ISBN 1-896522-27-0
Progressive Rock	ISBN 1-896522-20-3	Glam	ISBN 1-896522-26-2
Heavy Metal	ISBN 1-896522-47-5	Women In Rock	ISBN 1-896522-29-7

For ordering information see our web site at
www.cgpublishing.com